WHERE I LEFT MY PANTIES

BY ANDREANA MCCALL

TRUE PERSPECTIVE
PUBLISHING HOUSE

I

Copyright © 2012 by Andreana McCall
Where I Left My Panties
Printed in the United States of America
ISBN 978-0-9859892-7-9

AUTOGRAPH PAGE

Autograph this book to a woman who is working on overcoming their past

ACKNOWLEDGEMENTS

I want to thank God my Father for never giving up on me, Jesus for rewriting my story so beautifully and The Holy Spirit for guiding my fingers. My concerted effort is to be pleasing in Your sight. I especially thank Kahjha, Jessani and Alonzo for enduring their mother while she is "under construction." I love each of you and I am so grateful that God counted me worthy to steward over your lives. My prayer is that each of you learn to live and love in a way that defies any evidence of pain in your life. I also thank my "style-icon" sister/editor, Joan M. Harris. Thank you for helping me to better articulate what The Lord put on my heart; your prayers and encouragement are a blessing to my life. Thank you, of course, Mr. Sean Cort for giving me the privilege of telling my story.

TABLE OF CONTENTS

INTRODUCTION

"WHY PANTIES?"

Panties. What to say about them? A woman's most intimate garment. Cute. Sexy. Girly. But what about dangerous? Exhausting? Un-useful? Un-comforting? Not exactly the words you might want to associate with such a personal item that has such a profound purpose. Did I say profound? Indeed I did. Panties are merely a covering for the actual intimate part of a woman. A sheer (or opaque—whatever floats your boat) means of protection from unwanted intruders. Protection from lint, dirt, germs, even people. A woman's choice of panty can be as unique as she. Some prefer TOTAL coverage.

Others prefer minimal to NO coverage at all. Still others like a little mystery to their mode of protection. I like mine cute but comfortable. Truthfully that's a good description of me—cute and comfy. My panties have saved me on occasion and have left me in dire detriment on another. You see, you have to understand why panties are so important to any woman. They are an assertion, or even an extension of herself. A woman expresses something of who she is in her panty selection. Some choose carefully and with wisdom. Others may choose haphazardly and just pick-up a pack of three-count at the nearest WalMart. In any case, that woman has made a selection of undergarment fitting to her likeness and demeanor—her character.

To say that panties are a covering for a woman's "private parts" is to say something about what is considered private to a woman while simultaneously saying that those private things need to be covered. The word "vagina," is so taboo in the world today we'd much rather not discuss such verbiage in reference to our womanly genitalia. Instead we defer to "nicer" terms such as "VA-JAY-JAY." But what does that fact say about who we are as women? We do not like to discuss our "private parts" or anything of intimate value to tell the whole truth, at least not in one another's company—sometimes. "Bedroom talk" is for just that, the BEDROOM. Why is that? I'm thirty-two years old and I'm still looking for the answer. We talk about our children. We talk about being in labor with said children down to the centimeters effaced of our cervix. But to speak openly about sex, masturbation and pornography is unheard of. Private parts. Uncovered.

Instead we take the panties of our busyness, church involvement, family dedication or relationships, and cover, seemingly forever, those private areas of our lives. Hid inconspicuously underneath our costumes for the day, onlookers are none the wiser about the sweaty, raw, unsavory nakedness that we'd rather not share with the world around us. And by now, our panties are threadbare, at best, from all the wear they get without being exchanged for a fresh pair. We take our coverings off only in the right circumstances. And some women will wear a pair until they fume with the putrid odor of her privacy that has not been properly cleansed.   Guilty over here.   Maybe I'm the only woman who will admit to having worn a pair of panties some three days in a row for lack of bathing for that long.   Marine Corps Bootcamp—nuff said. Let's get naked.

What is it that makes panties such a hot topic among men?   I believe men love to revel in the knowledge that a woman has bequeathed to him a tiny parcel of herself.   It is a well-known custom in many social sects to steal a pair of women's undies as an act of accomplishment or rite of passage. "Panty-raid" anyone?   Whatever the situation, men are fascinated by women's panties.   It's more than the erotic idea of a lady half-naked.   It's more than the bit of skin that is revealed. Even men know that a woman places a certain importance on her panties.

She doesn't just undress in front of a man and reveal her intimates on a casual level—unless, of course, such behavior happens to denote certain elements of vocation for said woman (there is no judgment here).   Ordinarily, there are certain circumstances and prerequisites that must be met in order for such to take place.   A woman knows that in baring herself completely she is allowing a man to see her in a way that is a stark contrast to who she is while clothed.   Dressed—clad in undergarments—naked; the transition from one state to the next is important to take note of.   It is worth something to us that men recognize the care in which we take in order to reveal that final layer of clothing leading (hopefully for some random man) to utter nudity.

Some women will gladly strip down before a group of other women in certain circumstances. Gym class. Doctor's visit. Giving birth. It is a common thing we women do in the presence of one another—sometimes. We bar no holds. We hold no punches. We bare all—given the right conditions of course. We strip ourselves in front of each other to show that we accept one another and to hopefully gain a level of acceptance with each other. We'll also take it all off to show that we are comfortable in our own skin.

On occasion, however, there will always be the few stragglers who feel awkward with their nudity in the presence of other women. You remember "that one girl" who had to change clothes in the bathroom stall after PE class. She did not feel the safety to undress without the threat of mistreatment from those of like status to her own. Women. And as a grown up girl, that young lady, whoever she is right now, is probably still embarrassed by her own nakedness.

Women have been known to leave panties in sundry places. On the floor. On the bed. In the bathroom. In the hands of a man. Personally, I have left many a pair in the back pocket of a guy. That's right. It's a sort of game that I played. In exchange for hours (and in most cases minutes) of pure ecstasy, quite often my token of appreciation was my signature item of discretion. Several times (more than I care to share) I have played that game. A man came calling, we courted (or not), we had sex and to show my gratitude I'd give him the nights wages. A pair of my passion soaked intimate garments. In common slang "the draws," "the panties". He earned them, might as well keep them. Why? To remember me. To remember this event. To forever gaze upon those lacy thongs and think of the token I gave to him that night. The piece of myself that I willingly relinquished because I thought he was worth it. Not my husband. Not even my friend in many cases.

But a man to whom I wanted to give something, a piece of me (as if "the piece" he had just had wasn't good enough). And secretly, a man from whom I desired to receive something in return. Consequently, all I could muster was my panties. That's how I thought I wanted to be remembered; cold and crusted over from passion, balled up indiscreetly and tucked in his back pocket. That's a metaphor for my life if ever I have used one.

What made me do it? Horny? Yes. Lonely? Often. Wanting to relish in a bit of performance arrogance? Why not? But the real truth is that I thought I needed to give more than my body. And I had nothing more personal I wanted to share than those panties. They represented me for the moment. They had my essence upon them. They were just as much a part of me when worn as my skin. But at the same time, they were detachable, disposable. Useful. And to the male in whose possession they now found themselves: absolutely useless. That's how I felt early one morning after several hours of romping in a bed that was not my own, with a man to me unknown, in a room and not at home. Useless. Used. Less. *What am I doing? Here again? This again? What the hell?* As he tucked away my damp demure dainties, I cringed knowing that I had yet again left my panties in the hands of a stranger.

What now? All I know is that I left that room seemingly clothed. But completely void of covering. Void of what I really needed in order to remain safe. Void of something necessary for my protection. I was uncovered, and to the world around me I was dressed to the proverbial "nines". That's how it is when you give a piece of yourself away; no one else knows except you. Once we remove the covering to that "secret place" we are essentially saying, "You are worthy of knowing something about me that no one else is allowed to know." "You are worthy of my nakedness." The proper term for this type of knowledge is INTIMACY. In my immaturity and loneliness I settled for the sexual act in the place of true intimacy.

In giving that man my panties, let alone my body, I thought that somehow he would garner some intrinsic knowledge about my character and decide that I was the perfect woman for him. I fantasized about how "now our fate is sealed." Since I had shared the most private thing I can share with a man, certainly he was now obligated to receive ME. That's what my ultimate goal was. To be RECEIVED. To be accepted in the club of couple ship. The sad truth is that I knew all too well that my fancies were mere wishes of a childlike fixation to be joined to something or someone that I was not intended to be joined to—at least not in that particular manner. A soon forgot about experience rather than a lasting love affair with "the one." But that truth never stopped me from repeating this act of my will. That truth never settled within me and caused a change in my behavior. At least not until that particular night when I became ever so acutely cognizant of exactly where I was. And I'm not talking about the hotel room either.

In Genesis 2, The Bible teaches that Adam and Eve were breathed upon by God Himself and were given certain mandates within the parameters of their world which encompassed The Garden of Eden. But the most poignant truth for me from chapter 2 of Genesis is the very last verse, "They were naked and unashamed." To me, being naked and unashamed is saying a *whole* lot. After giving birth to three children (one by cesarean section), dealing with the effects of gravity and time on the female body, and of course hormones that rampage through my body at speeds greater than that necessary to break the sound barrier, and all of this once every single month of every single year—to be NAKED and also UNASHAMED...and please don't forget this...IN FRONT OF A MAN, means a whole lot more to me now than when I first read this story as a child. But I am forced to also remember that this was before "the fall" as it is commonly referred to by scholars and Christians alike. That is, before Adam and Eve partook of that which God had commanded them not to partake of. Before they sinned against

God, they were naked and unashamed in one another's presence.

So what happened? We all know the story. They ate THE FRUIT (not an apple as many people like to assume, for all we know it could've been a dragonfruit). And immediately "their eyes were opened and they knew that they were naked." I find it odd that the very first question by an all-knowing all-seeing God was, "Where are you?" You see, this was what God had asked me after my sex-capade. *Where are you?* All I knew was that I had just been with a man but I was the loneliest I had ever been. I knew that this man did not want to be my husband. I knew that this man may never have any further interest in me than what was going on between my legs. And that knowledge made me want to hide just like Eve.

Hide from myself and seemingly from God as well. But God and I were too acquainted for me to start hiding now. As I have studied this passage of scripture, I found that God didn't really ask them the first question in regard to their location, but as a matter of their state of mind. God knows all and sees all. He absolutely knew "where" they were. That is, where they were hiding. I'm sure He likewise knew "where" I was as well. Here I was, saved sanctified and sure enough filled with the Holy Ghost, yet I had just had sex with a man I was not married to—and to add insult to injury, it wasn't my first time in someone's bed without the covenant of marriage. Explain that, if you can.

XVIII

Even more intriguing to me than the first question God asked Adam and Eve, was the next question: "Who told you that you were naked?" When I read over this passage of scripture, I found that the question was ignored completely. "Who told you that you were naked?' No response. No address. No answer. Moving on to Adam blames Eve and Eve blames the serpent. In the end everybody involved has a price to pay, even the animal which availed himself to the use of the devil. God let no one off the hook for this one. But here lies the cataclysm for me; "who" indeed told them that they were naked? In my imagination I picture Adam and Eve partaking of this fruit together.

First—obviously—Eve, and soon afterwards, Adam. They are standing there together, condemned fruit in hand, and I must believe that mirrors had not been invented yet, so ultimately they were most likely looking at one another, beholding this change, this transformation that had taken place with one another after tasting this delectable piece of fruit. Eve is now very aware that Adam is different to say the least. And Adam, likewise, must try to fight off the overwhelming temptation to cover his eyes because what he is now beholding with the "naked eye" is a woman exposed.

So "who" told them they were naked? My answer: they told each other. I believe that their reaction to the opening of their eyes is what "told them" they were naked. But there remains yet another glitch; did nakedness even exist to them in the first place? I mean nakedness as we know it now. I have to believe that as we are now, we know the difference between being clothed and being naked. Well, clothing had not been invented until a few verses following the act of treason. So the only state they were accustomed to was nakedness. Bare. Nude. Normal. Nakedness was normal.

The fruit from the tree of "the knowledge of good and evil" had to come with fine print then. Not just "knowledge of good and evil," but *knowledge* in general had to be a byproduct of this fruit. I imagine the two of them gazing upon one another with that awkward silence we are all so keenly acquainted with when confronted with a question we know the answer to but also know the repercussions that await us if we give the answer.

In like manner, Adam and Eve, in my imagination, were confronted with each other's bare nakedness in a way they were not prepared to deal with. So I picture silence at the first. Weird glances here and there. I envision Adam as being repulsed or at least ashamed of Eve's nakedness once "their eyes were opened." What he had no misgivings about only seconds before had turned to something so abhorring it must now be covered up. After all, the very next thing they did after consuming corruption, was cover themselves.

I find it odd that the *knowledge* of nakedness moved Adam and Eve to desire a covering. They had been naked in front of each other for quite some time already. But suddenly, when they become *aware* that they are naked, they are no longer at peace or comfortable. Why was it so important to God to point out that while they were at peace with one another--meaning shalom, whole, nothing missing, broken or out of place--they were also UN-ashamed? What is it about being naked after the fall that causes shame? I believe it all comes down to panties-for me at least. Think about it; the first item of clothing Eve had to have made were nothing other than PANTIES. Face it girl, you can't do a whole lot of covering with fig leaves. She must have just covered what was necessary at the moment. It was God who made an entire outfit.

Panties must have importance then. Imagine the gutt-wrenching pain Eve had to feel after being blamed by Adam and never repented to. I don't find anywhere in the bible that Adam said something along the lines, "Look girl, my bad...I know WE were tricked by the serpent but I still love you. You are not at fault. As the head of this family I take full responsibility for what has occurred. Next time how about you and me talk before we talk to any more animals?" No such dialogue. So Eve is feeling not only the guilt of disobeying her Father, but also the guilt of being blamed for the whole "kit and kaboodle". What was she thinking when she heard those words fly out of Adams mouth like a runaway train, taking absolutely no part in the misdeed?

She follows suit and points the finger at the conductor of this carefully orchestrated play of sorrows, the serpent. And he wasn't doing much more talking once God showed up on the scene. Eve felt pressured to relieve herself of guilt by finding someone else to pass the buck to. And today, women are still living in the shadow of their own guilt and being imprisoned by someone else's discomfort with nakedness. I am such a woman.

So here we have: a man accusing his wife of the act that he willingly participated in, and a wife now defamed. But both were punished by God. Adam was punished with working himself to death. The bible declares "by the sweat of your brow will you have food to eat until you return to the ground from which you were made" (Genesis 3:19 NLT). Eve was given as a part of her punishment a longing after her husband. God says to Eve, "Your desire shall be for your husband" (Genesis 3:16 NKJV). My basic interpretation of this passage is that Eve was cursed to desire her husband, but he will be too consumed in tilling the very ground that brought damnation upon the earth to pay attention to her. Think about that; desire as a curse.

A researcher at heart, I had to find the meaning behind the words on the page. That particular word for "desire" is the Hebrew word *teshuka*; the literal meaning is "a longing and a stretching out after." It is used by God only two other times in the bible. There are literally only three mentions of this specific form of desire in the entire bible. We have the first one mentioned in reference to Eve. The next time it is mentioned is when God is talking with Cain and says to him, "sin *desires* to have you" (Genesis 4:7). The last time it is mentioned is in the book of Songs, or Song of Solomon, where the Shunamite woman declares "I am my beloved's and his *desire* is toward me" (Song of Solomon 7:10). Now this latter mention of the word is important to understand. What you must know is that Song of

Solomon not only speaks of a man and his lover or wife, but it is also a representation of Jesus and his relationship to the church. So as the woman declares that she belongs to her beloved, we can also say that she is declaring that she belongs to God. And because she belongs to GOD it is HIS desire that is toward her. Therefore, it can be concluded that a woman is cursed to desire a husband or a man in the same manner that sin desires to consume us as Christians and also in the same manner that God himself desires to save us from sin. Yeah, that's real deep for me too.

Not all desire is good then, to say the absolute least; and the curse of desire is such that we as women are left in a sick near sinful state, clawing after a man who has no real desire for us. Or at least the desire he has for us is not the twisted form that we have for him, because that was not a part of the curse brought onto the male species. Now I'm not saying that every woman has some ill form of treacherous desire for a man. But I am saying that according to what God pronounced over all female-kind, it is our nature to desire and long for a husband.

We do not have to be consumed by this sick desire and, in fact, when we accept Jesus into our hearts we become someone new. Please pay attention to what the bible says about being a "new creation". The bible specifically states "all things are BECOME new" (2 Corinthians 5:17). So then, it's not this automatic "now I'm saved and a new creation" type of thing. On the contrary, the wording suggests that the newness COMES, or, is in the process of BECOMING. Consequently, until we

XXIII

change our minds about ourselves and husbands and sin, that issue lies dormant within us.   And I'm convinced that even with changed minds and new hearts we have a tendency to crave the attention of a man.   I'm divorced as of many years ago, saved as of many years prior to that and YES, I too still desire the attention of a man.

This desire for a man's attention is subject to have its way with us, especially within those of us who have either been married and know what it's like to be with a man sexually, or those of us who have experienced sexual interaction with a man despite the institution of marriage.   We have to acknowledge that that particular internal struggle of Adamic-sin-nature, concerning the desire for a husband, is real and is present within us, and we have to be willing to address it at its core.   We have to be willing to deal with sexual sin in a real and relevant way that reaches women where they are.

In truth, we have to take off our self-prepared panties, get naked and stare into the mirror and behold our real selves, our raw selves, our un-dressed-up selves.   Who we are at our most vulnerable state is who God wants to really see and deal with.   It's who I need to deal with in order to be the real person God wants me to be.   And I will tell you right now, NO–it is not easy.   No—it is not comfortable.   And NO, it doesn't feel good.   I wish I could also tell you that there were some kind of remedy or three-step program that will take the "hornies" away and you'll never be the same.   I wish I could tell you that if you keep going to church and trusting God that "everything is gonna be alright" and you will be free from sexual sin for the rest of your days. It's not that simple. That's not my story. And I got a hunch that it may not be the story of many a young CHRISTIAN lady.

I am in no way minimizing the role of the church. I believe that church is important in the life of a Christian. However, I also believe that church is not enough. I have been in church most of my life and as a saved, Holy Ghost filled WOMAN in her thirties I STILL fall into sexual sin. Is it my intent to just sleep with a man and get my fix? Absolutely not. And sometimes--being very honest here--absolutely yes. Like any person struggling to overcome a bad habit, some days I'm good and other days not so much. I believe that this desire, this urge of my flesh is a form of addiction.

I also believe that there is freedom, and that such freedom comes from engaging several factors simultaneously and consistently. But I can't say that I have experienced that freedom completely yet. And I am not writing to give you a plan of action either, but rather to share my struggles—some victories and some losses—and maybe offer some comfort to someone who may be struggling in the way that I AM. For me, this is my thorn to endure.

I believe with everything that is within me God allows some of us to maintain certain sin issues in our lives just so that we must rely on Him. Also, so that we don't get beside ourselves thinking we have arrived. You are not obligated to agree with me on this. I know what it feels like to go years without having sex with a man and not even have the accustomed longing of my flesh that would lead to an occasional wet-dream. I know what it feels like to not have a desire for a man in my life, to be content and not shaken when the finest thing God ever made walks up on me, flashes a gorgeous smile and proceeds to launch a futile attempt to get me into bed.

But I also know what it feels like to be so lonely at night that I have ventured to pornographic websites to mentally escape the depression of not having a mate. I know what it feels like to engage in masturbation to alleviate the craving of my body and my personal desire to be touched. I also know what it feels like to deal with the simultaneous guilt and regret from having engaged in those shameful acts. I know what it feels like to let down my guard and set aside my standards because I just wanted a man to love me for the moment.

I know what it feels like to be heartbroken to the point of nearly being through with God Himself. I know what it feels like. I'm not proud of it all. But I feel the need to let some woman know YOU ARE NOT ALONE. That's why I'm writing this. And it all starts with panties. My panties. Your panties. It starts with where we left our panties.

Chapter 1

Taking My Panties off

f I'm going to be so bold as to talk about panties, I must qualify myself by taking my own off in front of you so that I'm not talking about things that I heard about or read somewhere, but things I have lived and am now living. Where to begin? In order to understand where I am now, you have got to know where I came from. I will start with the realization of my brokenness.

By the end of 2005, I was at an all-time low in my life. I had been hurt by my family, hurt by the church, hurt by friends, hurt by men.   You name it, and I've probably been through it. I didn't know a person could hurt so much and still be sane, let alone alive. Lied on by friends that I loved dearly. Deceived by members of the church I devoted my life to.   Cast out by my family—literally, I was put out on the street with my children in tow by close relatives.   Rejected by my mother. Rejected by men. All a sista wanted was to be loved by someone.   I just wanted to know that someone loved me and that I was loveable. It doesn't feel too good being dissed by absolutely everyone that you love—all at the same time.   Not good at all.

I carried that feeling of emptiness and hurt with me into the next year.   2006 found me even further in the pit of oppression.   Trying to figure out who was for me and who was against me.   And the latter group seemed to be on the winning team.   So, on a trip to the mall one spring day that year, feeling especially not-good about myself, a tall handsome young man paid me a compliment.   "You are so beautiful," he said to me taking my hand and looking me square in the eyes to the point that I drew back.

It may seem small and insignificant to you, but when you have been devastated by life and the last thing on your mind has to do with how you look to the world, a well-timed, well-placed compliment can just make your day—heck—make your life better for the moment.   I needed that compliment that day.   *"To the hungry soul every bitter thing is sweet"* that's what the bible says in Proverbs 27:7.   And my soul was famished. Perhaps a person should not be so moved by a mere compliment as I was that day, but feeling unloved by people can run you ragged and cause you to overvalue things that are superficial. Being treated unjustly by people you have done nothing but go out of your way for, can make you feel like crap (and not the censored type), just speaking plainly.   And the battle of a Christian, as I have learned (and am still learning), is to rise above the manure people throw on you and still see the light of day.   My eyes must have been closed.

Anyway, this young man and I started dating. Truthfully, I was only interested in how he could make me forget that my world was crumbling around me.   I knew that I wanted to sleep with this man the moment he engaged me at the mall. I might as well paint an accurate picture for you.   No use lying or dressing up the truth now.   I was tired of hurting.   I was tired of fighting with life and always feeling like I was losing the battle.   I was tired of being lied to by church folks who I thought meant well, but ended up being more harmful to me than the devil himself (OK maybe not as bad as the enemy but pretty doggone close).   I was tired of doing all I knew to do and still coming up short.   I was just tired.   I wanted relief from the pain.   I wasn't into drugs.   And I wasn't into drinking. So an orgasm seemed like a suitable outlet for me at the time.

We had nothing in common.   After a few dates, I invited him home with me and we had sex.   Not even mind blowing, memorable sex either—just sex.   I will never forget what happened DURING this sexual experience.   Brace yourself, it's about to get real...well, just *real*.   As I lay on top of

3

this man, I literally heard the voice of God say to me, "Is this what you really want?" And, knowing the voice of God, I answered (not audibly of course because that would have been a little too "awkward") "No it's not." I wish I could tell you that I got off of that guy, kicked him out and started praising The Lord. Sorry, that's not what happened. I continued in this act of sin. I felt so sorrowful afterwards though—a sorrow that I had never known after having committed some sinful act. Something was different about this experience.

Well, I later found out that I was pregnant. Here's the funny part: I was on the pill and we DID use a condom. That's the whole truth and nothing but. I was so ashamed of myself. Just a year and a half earlier I had preached for the first time (yep—you read that right—in a church in a pulpit in front of a sizable congregation—I HAD PREACHED—several times in fact). I had established myself as a praise dancer and praise team leader. I was definitely an influential part of my church. To put it to you short, I was not in "baby Christian" status. But honestly, does that really matter? Anyway, I knew The Word. As a matter of fact, I was even mentoring a young teenage mother at the time. Of course I knew and know Jesus and His voice. But none of that was enough to stop me from entering into this downward spiraling fuselage.

The church that I was a part of did not cast me out and make me feel more ashamed. On the contrary, they tried to embrace me and make me feel as comfortable as I did when I would teach Sunday-School. On the inside of myself, however,

I could not bear to keep up a look of holiness while feeling like a slut. Aside from my personal torment of shame, God was leading me away from this church for other reasons that will most likely take up another book in the very near future.

The tension of shaky, lopsided relationships that I had been engaged in with key members of this church, coupled with trying to fight off personal wounds from these members, and also dealing with the fact that the father of this child vanished when he found out I was pregnant only made me feel more ashamed. So I left that church. I took a few months away from church entirely because I was so beat down by life.

I seriously nearly lost my mind. I remember sitting in my room watching the walls around me move and change shapes and little creeping things go up and down them. I would hear whispers in my ear. I was literally losing my mind. I would lie on the floor with the blanket covering my head "hiding" from the world around me. How I managed to take care of my six and seven year old daughters at that time is beyond me. It was on such a day that I broke down in the middle of my living room floor while my girls were at school. I screamed and cried until my nose started to drip with blood.

I was in complete vexation of my soul. I don't even think I had the presence of mind to pray at this time of pouring out. I just cried like I had never cried before in my life over anything. It was literally several hours before I pulled myself up. But when I got up I heard God say, "This was your time to mourn all the loss you've had—now leave it here." God showed me how I had never cried over the loss of my marriage. It was a screwed-up mess of a marriage, but it still represented a loss for me.

I never mourned the loss of all my friendships (even the crappy ones that meant me no good whatsoever). I hadn't even mourned the loss of my father that had occurred only five years prior and was still fresh in my mind at this time. God told me very clearly that all loss—ANY loss—needs to be mourned. In the hustle and bustle of life as a single parent to two children, having lost my father who I was very close to, striving to maintain cordial relations with people who selfishly wounded and crippled me, dealing with "frenemies", being pregnant by a man I did not know nor knew where he was, and just trying to stay sane, keep my head above the water and continue living; I had no time to mourn. But when I got up from that crying episode, I knew I was different. Like Jacob, I knew I had just wrestled with God.

I decided to keep the baby I was pregnant with (yes I considered abortion to the point of being in an abortion clinic). The fact that the father was MIA didn't bother me as much. I even started to get along with my girls' father. I was experiencing deliverance like I never had before. Still a little apprehensive about church, I was not yet ready to return. I would get my church fix from television and by spending personal time with God. He just began to reveal Himself to me in the most amazing ways. I found a way to pay my tithes through sponsoring several African children and partnering with televised ministries. However, I knew that my absence from a physical church was merely for a season, and God wanted me to be connected to a local church. I later found one to attend.

I was soaring in spiritual highs. But the icing on the cake for me was that my desire for men and sex was sated. I mean, I was literally—in my mind—over men. Over the midnight "sweats" (those times when my body was aching to be penetrated). Over the affinity I had developed for pornography, and over the secret self-satisfying I had been doing for years. I had a resolve that made me feel invincible. I was walking with God in high places and receiving revelation after revelation; I just knew God had delivered me from death and a lifestyle of killing myself slowly. I was so grateful to be free of sexual desire. For the first time, I was the conqueror and not the conquered, and all I could do was praise Jesus. I considered all of my issues with sex and men conquered and dealt with. And for the moment, they genuinely were.

The church that I mentioned I had started attending was new and exciting to me, and I wanted to get involved as soon as I could. I was looking for some friends I could share God's word with and maybe have bible study with. I just wanted to be connected. Well, what I found was a "singles ministry" that was not exactly suited for my particular brand of singleness. Being a parent as well as a single person added an interesting dynamic to my ability to "connect" with the singles of this new church. They would have "singles events" but my children

7

were not allowed to come. They would even have "singles bible study" that my children were also not permitted to attend with me. And on the rare occasion I was permitted to bring my children to singles' events, I was not engaged by anyone and pretty much isolated as everyone had their own particular clique to mingle with. I began to notice this trend early on. At first I was unmoved by it. God and I were doing our *thang* and I was in such a high spiritual place that I could not be shaken—even from the obvious injustice I was receiving from this church.

I could literally hear in my spirit what many of the congregants were thinking about me. It was evident that I was unmarried. It was evident that I had two children while pregnant with a third. What was not conspicuous to them is that I genuinely had a private spiritual life. What was not obvious to them is that I was taking care of my family financially without government assistance (at this particular time anyway); I was gainfully employed. I was just a single mother in love with Jesus looking to share my faith with others. Instead of embracing me and making me feel accepted, I was told I could not participate in certain ministerial opportunities.

I tried to join certain ministries and was told I could not because I was not married. I shook those offenses off like water. I noted them and made a critical determination about this particular church. But I did not let those offenses deter me from coming to church and being fed spiritually. And after several conversations with the pastors of the church I was finally allowed to at least join the prayer team.

***What does this have to do with leaving your panties in
some man's back pocket?*** Glad you asked. What is important
to note here is that God had done a serious work of deliverance
in my life. I was genuinely living this Christian life we are
called to live. That's not to say I was perfect; I still had some
sidebar issues that God was also working on. But at a crucial
point in my spiritual growth, I was in a church that would not
support me in the area of my singleness. Or better stated: they
did not have an adequate system in place for singles. There
were no opportunities for me to be uniquely ministered to.

There were no opportunities for me to genuinely be an
active part of the church since I was unable to join certain
ministries. I was basically made to feel left out of many church
events that claimed to be focused on the family. To add to my
sense of isolation, whenever anyone was speaking about "the
family" all I would hear was "husbands" and "wives". Never a
mention made about single parents. I was made to feel like I
was not a part of a unit or team; I certainly didn't feel like I was a
part of a family. I needed interaction with people. I needed
to be connected to others in a way that gave me a replacement
for the lack of companionship in my life.

I believe that those ingredients are essential to single
people maintaining a lifestyle of singleness apart from sexual sin.
Being in a church that has no support for singles is one element
that I believe can either aide in the fall of a single person or
hinder them from maintaining a level of freedom from sexual

sin.   There are more elements that I will discuss in more detail later in this book.

I remember reaching out to the first lady of the church with my concerns about ministering to singles.   I was told, "We can't make relationships happen."   While I understand that there is some truth in that, I also believe that people at church need to be more sensitive to the lives of single parents.   Single parenting is a brand of singleness very unlike being single without children.   Single parents don't have it easy by any measure.   We have to do absolutely everything that needs to be done in our families on our own.

Many people will say and have said, "You're never alone with God."   That's a great spiritual truth, but being very honest, I AM ALONE.   I have to: check homework, cook dinner, fix the car, do hair, do laundry, go fuss at teachers, fuss at kids, go grocery shopping, buy school clothes, pay for braces, pay the bills, clean the house, clean the car, keep the kids clean, keep myself clean, fix whatever breaks around the house, attend parent-teacher conferences for multiple children at multiple locations at multiple times, take the kids to the doctor, take the kids to the dentist, pick the kids up from school when they're sick, miss work/school for picking the kids up from school, haggle with employers about shifts and hours, bargain babysitters for extended hours, bring kids to school with me because there is no childcare or school on certain days for the children but there is still school for me—and this is just the normal day-to-day stuff.   So when I'm at church what I really need is a high five. A pat on the back for getting my butt out of bed, my kids dressed and making it to the sanctuary ON TIME (occasionally).

That's truth people may not want to hear. And many churches do not offer much support to single parents. You want to know what single parents really need? We need money—yeah I said it, deal with it. Pay some single parent's bills for a FEW MONTHS without them having to ask for help. Get some single parent's car fixed. Help single parents move. Watch the children of single parents for a few weekends for FREE. Take single mothers to a spa and have their homes cleaned for them. Prepare dinner for a single parent for several days. These are some support efforts that can be put into place to actually help single parents. Sadly, not many people are willing to offer this kind of support. Don't wait for singles and single parents to ask for help; simply avail yourself to them.

Many will say, "Just grin and bear it-what doesn't kill you only makes you stronger," or my all-time-favorite, "Endure hardships as a good soldier." Yeah, all of that is true and good, but the real truth is that it gets old—quickly. It is frustrating ALL THE TIME. It is lonely ALL THE TIME. And all of it is happening ALL THE TIME. To attend a church that has no interest in my single life or single issues is another fight that only adds to my ongoing battle with life. To attend a church where the congregants are unfriendly and uncompassionate towards me and my single parenthood is really heartbreaking.

11

Now that I've got that out, let me continue. Here I was, newly delivered from sexual sin, and in a church that was not interested in helping me sustain the deliverance that God had brought to my life. Of course, the church had no idea what I had been delivered from, but they were not interested in learning either. The bottom line is that there was no genuine ministry available to me as a single parent, and no one taking steps toward me as a new member of the church.

Now, apart from that phenomenon, I had some critical personal issues to deal with as well (emphasis on "critical"). I would see other single parents and try to mingle with them, but something would rise up on the inside of me letting me know that they were not doing singleness the way that *I* was doing singleness. Call it discernment if you like. I knew that I was serious about the things of God. I was not on the fence by any measure. My weekends were spent with my children and with my bible and a notepad. I developed a sort of distancing myself apart from *those singles*. To put it in terms of true understanding, I began to judge some of the single women I came into contact with at church.

Some seemed genuinely interested in developing and maturing in Christ, others had predetermined ideas about me as a single parent, and still others I merely wrote off because I felt myself spiritually superior to them. I knew God had delivered me from my sexual struggle and "if they really wanted to be healed, they would let God heal them too." Sound familiar to anyone?

12

God had allowed me to discern that there were single women at my church struggling with sexual sin as I had struggled. He wanted me to be aware of a need that I was uniquely suited to meet. Instead of taking that opportunity to let my heart weep for them and encourage them, I took what God had let me in on and let it harden my heart against them. The whole story is kind of ironic. I was a single parent being secretly and overtly scrutinized, yet at the same time I was scrutinizing and being critical of others that were in the same state that I had formerly found myself in—and not too long beforehand.

At first, I tried to offer some guiding principles to the single women I eventually found myself connected to. I would make attempts to show them that I knew what they were going through. It never crossed my mind that while I was doing that, I was probably making them feel uncomfortable and even more ashamed. My line of thinking was: "You're broken and I know how to fix you." But that was not what God would have had them to know, certainly not in the manner that I was approaching the issue. *"There is a way that seems right to a man but the end thereof are the ways of death;"* that's what Proverbs 16:25 says. My way of reaching out to women that I thought were "worse off" than me was not the way God would have had me to reach out to them—at least not with me thinking in the background "if you really want to be delivered you can be". That's judgment. That was me setting myself up in the position of "sexual sin guru". And I am not. I was zealous for what God had done for me, no doubt, but that did not make me the expert on all things sexual sin related. What God had shown to me I was somehow unable to offer to others—mercy.

How many of you know that God will allow you to really get a taste of someone else's life if you think you are infallible? Well I know personally that He does that. In my heart, I had erred against some of the single women I was in contact with. I know that deep down I meant well, but the practical aspect of putting my intents into proper godly action was not something I was acquainted with at that time.

But God was going to reveal to me in a very personal way what these women really needed. You see, when you're standing on the mountaintop looking down on everybody else, you're really only postured for one inevitable event—falling, or at least a trip down the mountainside.

For the next four years following 2006 I maintained my chastity. I was approached by men and was completely unmoved by them. I simply was not interested in having a boyfriend. Not that I didn't find any of them attractive, but I was content—for the moment. I developed some genuine connections to other single women. I tried to urge some of them to "live free of sexual sin" without their permission to speak along those lines. I imposed my ideas of freedom on them, without genuinely understanding where they were. I thought I had the answer to their problems—Jesus . . . right??

Because I was genuinely not thinking about men, the devil took the opportunity to seize upon me. The devil may not know everything as God does, but trust me when I tell you this: he knows your phone number, your email address, your physical address, your MYSPACE page, your FACEBOOK page, your TWITTER feed—let's just say the devil knows pertinent information about YOU—and he certainly knows a heap of info about me too. After all, he's been around for thousands of years, and from the moment you were born he's been watching your every move. He knows what you like, what you detest, what gives you goose-bumps.

Please believe me when I say, the devil knows a whole lot about you. Well, I wasn't paying attention to what he knew about me. When the enemy saw that I was not being moved by "any-ole-man", he went to work cooking up one suited to my exact specifications. He—the enemy—might be old and defeated but he certainly is not stupid, and should not be underestimated.

In 2009, I had reconnected with an "old friend". If ever there was a man to move me, he was it. The devil knew that, and somehow, I did NOT. Well, I remained my sanctified self for a few months of our acquaintance. Then, the inevitable happened. You know how your heart starts to imagine the fantasy. The "what-ifs" began to kick in and I found myself falling in love for the first time in a very long time. My heart was delighted at the possibility of realizing the dream of being FOUND. The bible says in Proverbs 18:22 (KJV), *"Whoso*

15

findeth a wife findeth a good thing. . ." With that in mind, I thought this was my opportunity to be found. Indeed, that's what I wanted. Indeed, that's what I thought I was leading up to. I was so excited at the thought that God was finally answering my heart's desire to be married again. You see, while I was in my "delivered" state I had never stopped desiring to be married, only to not be conflicted in my body while unmarried.

Well, I had been out of the dating game for many years. I had been out of the company and influence of men for equally a number of years. And let me also inform you that this was a long distance acquaintance. I had no idea what I was really doing, so I thought it was OK to go it alone. I thought I could handle myself in a relationship (or something like it). Boy oh boy was I wrong. This "relationship" brought things out of me that I didn't know were still inside of me. Insecurity? Check. Flesh rising again? Check. Renewed awareness of my former phallic fixation? Giant check in size double XL please.

My first thoughts were, *Thank you God for hearing the cry of my heart!* I was grateful to God and wanted to be cautious as to not place this man in God's place in my life. I was well aware of the dangers of making a man my idol. At least, I thought I was. I tried to keep the things of God before me. It was not easy.

Being wooed by a man for the first time in a very long time can be captivating. There is a certain freedom and confidence that comes when the answer to the question: "Am I still desirable?" is answered emphatically affirmative by a man's pursuit. Here's the real issue: this was THEE man, in my eyes. He was everything that I loved in a man—handsome, genuine, reserved demeanor, masculine and YES—he was a Christian.

Let's just say: whatever your particular fantasy of THE ONE happens to be, this man was all of that to me and then some. To make things a little more interesting, I had a history with him—high school sweethearts nearly engaged after graduation—you guessed it, he was my first love (you have to understand the gravity and depth of this acquaintance).

I was flattered by the prospect of a relationship with a man I was somewhat acquainted with already. I was falling without a net, hopefully, into the heart of this man. What I was feeling for him seemed to be reciprocated to me. I remember thinking, "This is too easy and too perfect to be real." Sure enough, it was. Because my heart was so aflutter with new feelings, I was blind to the clues that things were going awry. Well, maybe not altogether blind, but certainly a lot less attentive.

We began having very sexual conversations that ultimately led to outright phone sex. At first, I would reign myself back in and tell him, "Look we cannot go there!" You see, when you start to engage that space of attraction coupled with intimacy, it is natural that sexual desire would follow. However, not having any "reigns" to pull back on can lead you in a danger zone that is difficult to get out of.   And this sista was in a sticky rat trap.

As the weeks progressed into months of communicating with "old friend," I became less uncomfortable with our steamy chats.   By the turn of the new-year, my heart was so open, and my hopes were so high.   I just knew that it was only a matter of time and "we were going to be married anyway," I would think to myself, "So why not explore this area of our relationship?"   I wanted him to know that WHEN he decided to marry me, he would be satisfied sexually.   There was a part of me that wanted to let him know that I was a sexual being very comfortable in my sexuality.   Yes, even as a Christian woman.

And if I were to be very honest (as if I'm going to stop now while I'm on hot jelly roll), I think that's an OK line of thinking in the context of relationships.   But herein lies a particular problem, we were NOT even in a real relationship. We were in that popular place of being "friends" and no commitment had been voiced.   Let me tell the whole truth; no discussion of an authentic relationship between me and him had even taken place.

So for all of my intentions of informing him about who I was as a sexual being, I was still losing a critical battle in a major way. We should have been more focused on the direction of our acquaintance than on how sexual we both were.   That line of discussion should take place within the confines of a genuine relationship seriously moving toward walking down the aisle.

And who was there to tell me THAT? And if they were to tell me, with my heart all aflutter, and my body all aflame, do you really think I was going to listen?

I was carrying on with this man in a sexual manner like we were married already and we weren't even technically together. We weren't even in the same state. Whenever Boaz does find me, of course I want to be able to satisfy him sexually and I expect him to be able to satisfy me sexually. I don't think that such discourse is out of line nor unchristian. I do believe that such discussion should be reserved for aforementioned RELATIONSIP status, but also, such discussion should take place among women and men, especially among Christians in church. I see far too many marriages being ravaged by the enemy in the area of sex.

I am convinced that more women need to know that sexual gratification is not of the devil. Yes, it should be reserved for the covenant of marriage if it is going to be a blessed experience, but the truth of the matter is that every single woman is not going to wait. Correction, every single CHRISTIAN woman is not going to wait. I know this because I am a single woman who happens to be a Christian who is having a hard time waiting. I suffer because of it. I know I'm not going to hell because of it. Yet, I also know that my life is a lot more difficult because I oftentimes choose not to hold out and reserve sexual gratification for the marriage bed. But I believe in my heart that God is not unaware of my struggle. I believe that He knows how difficult the meantime can be (and believe me it's

MEAN)—that time of waiting to be found by a man. I also believe that He extends a special measure of grace for women such as me. Again, I say, you are not obligated to agree.

Let me get back to me and "old friend". He and I were "just friends". "Just friends" who would occasionally engage in phone-sex. "Just friends" who really did discuss the possibility of marriage between us on few occasions. "Just friends" who were enjoying the renewal of an old former relationship. We were ONLY just friends.

I was willing to engage this man on certain levels of intimacy because we had been there before. There was no other man I felt more comfortable with. No other man I thought knew me through and through. There was no other man with whom I felt safe enough so as to not need boundaries—those "reigns" I discussed earlier. Pay attention to that last sentence; in fact, reread it. Now, I need you to pause and SELAH on that for a spell.

Thank you. Let me tell you this: when the devil sets a trap, he sets a trap. I needed you to pause and carefully consider what I had just said because I think many of us women know what it feels like to be in a comfortable place with a man. That place where we feel like we can let go and settle in a little bit because there seems to be no threat to our security, that's where I was—feeling unthreatened, in love and not wanting it to end.

I also felt that if I didn't maintain this man's attention he would not want anything else to do with me. So I allowed myself to continue entertaining phone sex with him. I allowed myself to pretend we had something that we did not have. I played this game of "one day maybe he'll commit to me" not even considering the possibility that he would not. Since I had no other offers of a relationship, I settled for a frame in place of the portrait. And you can't build a foundation on ground that hasn't even been broken.

While I was building something in my mind, he was content to allow things to remain as they were between us—shallow. While I was erecting for myself this fantasy that ended with the two of us at the alter jumping over a broom, the reality was that "old friend" was unaware of my heart's urgency because I wasn't making any real attempts to bring him up to speed. Afraid that my desires would be perceived as desperation, I relented to just wait it out. Bide my time and pretend to be this "mature" woman who was capable of navigating through a man's indifference (delusional, I know—but remember I had been out of the dating game for a **significant** amount of time).

I soon became anxious to make our acquaintance an official relationship. Instead of voicing these concerns to him in a rational manner, for fear of rejection, I silently acquiesced to engaging him on this superficial level of relating. With no established boundaries in place, I found myself getting upset about things that wouldn't bother me before. He wouldn't call and I would work myself into a frenzy thinking *Oh no! He doesn't want to be with me*—silently torturing myself with what ifs. This anxiety was heightened by the fact that this was a long distance thing. I was feeling extremely insecure. Here I was; trying to build something out of nothing with this man that I was genuinely in love with, pretending not to notice his cues of waning interest, while simultaneously trying to parent all three of my children.

In addition to that, I was also dealing with the lust of my body returning stronger than ever, while attempting to maintain a spiritual connection to God and make it all look pleasant. I was open prey for the enemy. And I was open prey to myself. How many of you know that your mind will create an alternate reality for you, in which all of your fears seem to be coming true? The enemy was moving in like a flood, and I was too busy to notice.

I thought I was this confident Christian woman who knew who she was and what she wanted and what she stood for, yet through this situation with a man from my past, the cracks in my character began to show. I had never realized how really insecure I really was until this episode with "old friend". While I was genuinely intending not to turn him into an idol, somewhere in the course of our pseudo-relationship he became one. Not only him, but the idea of being in a relationship with the prospect of marriage itself became an idol to me. I was constantly fixating on what our lives would be like as a "real" couple. I wondered how my children would relate to him as their step-father. I wondered how his children would relate to me as their step-mother. I was one daydreaming chick.

The truth of the matter is: having those feelings and those desires is NOT sinful. Thinking about a future with a man is nothing to be ashamed of, or feel awkward or out-of-place about. But when those feelings become the central part of your mental faculties and your attention is more on those feelings than anything else, you have now exalted them to a place of importance that supersedes God's importance in your life. Those feelings and desires have become an idol. An idol is anything that you devote your time, attention and affections toward. Because you devote your time, attention and affections toward something that is not God, you are, in a sense, worshipping something other than God.

And God says very plainly in Exodus 34:14, *"thou shall worship no other god . . . for The Lord is a jealous God."* That means that God desires to have the centermost seat of our affections, time and attention. So when we give more attention to our feelings and desires (or ANYTHING else for that matter), we exalt them above God. Those feelings and desires can then begin to lead us into behaviors that oppose God.

All of this happens seemingly unawares to us. It sure was an unaware happening in my life. I looked up one day, and I was carried away with my feelings for a man and my desire to be married. I let my desire to be with a man lead me into having phone-sex with a man I wasn't even in a relationship with. I let my desire to be with a man restrict me from setting appropriate boundaries and engaging in healthy conversation about my future with a man. I let my *desire* rule and consume me—just like Eve. It all happened so quietly and subtly that I completely lost myself to it. And before I was completely aware of myself, I was standing before God naked and quite ashamed. I am still recovering even as I write this.

By now, I'm sure you're wondering, "so when exactly did you give this dude your panties?!" I promise I'm getting to that, just keep reading.

Off in "La-La Land," I was an utter mess. I was sexually frustrated because I so desired this man, emotionally frustrated because he was not making any attempt to really commit to me, mentally frustrated by my need to figure out why he was taking so long, and spiritually frustrated because I no longer felt God's presence like I had before. Add all of this to the fact that life for me did not slow down—I still had three children to take care of, school to concentrate on and church to attend.

With so much stress going on around me and inside of me, I found myself returning to pornography and masturbation. With my sexual desire so aroused, I needed something to take the edge off. I couldn't have actual sex with this man, so I casted him in the starring role of my mental sexcapade. When my mind ran out of intriguing material, I ventured to pornography to resupply myself with ample juicy imagery. The guilt I felt from engaging in these activities wasn't enough to make me stop. Loneliness was the chief driver of my self-made escape vehicle. I was trying to get away from it all—escape from life. Escape from fears of perpetual loneliness. Escape

24

from the mental awareness that things were not going as planned with me and "old friend." Pornography and masturbation became my escape mechanisms.

What started off as a quaint rekindling of an old-flame soon began to turn into a flicker from a dying match. The momentum of our acquaintance died down to the point we were barely in contact on regular basis—at least, not as regular as I expected. Let me remind you, I hadn't had the faintest scent of a man in my immediate proximity for several years. So I assumed that we would be in some form of regular communication.

I don't know—something along the lines of once a week seemed reasonable to me. My thinking was: if a man is interested, he will naturally want to talk with me. So when "old friend" seemed to be playing dodge-ball with my calls, I found myself becoming very ill at ease. I saw his no-call policy as him distancing himself from me and I didn't understand why. I had no clue about the dating-game version 2010.0. Instead of engaging in adult conversation about my feelings and where our "relationship" was going, I blew up and ended whatever it was we were doing. This left me unsettled and even more insecure.

Here I was with my feelings and body all aroused like they hadn't been in a long time. For four years, the smell of a man (and I LOVE the smell of a man as he passes by—my version of the "new car scent"), wouldn't so much as cause me to turn my head. Then, seemingly out of nowhere, "old friend" shows up wrapped in all of my childhood dreams of happily-ever-after, and I'm a flat-out wreck. Even though I had ended things with this man, I didn't stop the masturbation or the pornography. I was powerless. My heart was crushed. My hopes were destroyed. I was hurt. I was lonely and I had no other outlet.

I had no other escape to mentally numb myself from life around me and the pain inside me—the pain of life as a single parent and then the pain of rejection on top of that. The result was an anxious, insecure, depressed, angry woman constantly on edge, constantly needing a "fix". And to top it all off, my spiritual life had nearly come to a complete standstill. Not a full stop, but a definite snail-pace.

I remember asking God, "Why is this happening to me? Why now?" And He reminded me of a prayer I had prayed about this acquaintance before things started heating up. I said, "God I love him. But, if this is not your will for me, close this door and shut it fast! Even if it means I will be hurt, I would rather have Your will for my life than what I think I need." I will never forget praying that prayer. And I meant every single word of it. So I took the situation with this man as God showing me that He was shutting this door. At first, I was OK with the idea of God leading me in a different direction, but then, I started to feel lonely and guilty. Lonely because for so many years I had not been in anything remotely close to a relationship, and this episode with "old friend" reminded me of the companionship my heart really longed to share with someone.

Guilty because I felt like I had done this man an injustice in the way that I had treated him due to my own insecurities. I was oblivious to the law of reciprocity. Instead of looking at both sides of the coin, I focused all my attention on what I thought I had done wrong—a trademark of insecurity.

With all of my guilt and loneliness, I tried to reach out to "old friend". I tried to apologize and make things "right" again. But I got nothing from him—absolutely nothing. I was devastated by his unwillingness to communicate with me at all. I was hurt, confused and desperate. Confused, because deep down I knew that I had compromised myself in major ways with this guy, yet he was treating me like I was the one who had betrayed him. Desperate, because I began to wonder if he was my only chance at love. I began to wonder if I had just blown things out of proportion because of my own insecurities.

In my insecure mind, I absorbed within myself all the responsibility of what had happened between us. And that is a dangerous thing to do. Insecurity will cause you to devalue yourself and see the world through a dirty lens—a world where guilt consumes you every time you make a mistake. In the world that I had created in my insecure mind, I had done everything wrong with this man and he had been the innocent bystander. Guilt was eating me alive—not only the misplaced guilt of a screwed up pseudo-relationship, but also the guilt of my indulgence in masturbation and pornography. All of this while trying to maintain some semblance of a relationship with God. I was unable to find my place in Him again through the

27

shame caused by continuing to indulge in masturbation and pornography, as well as the misplaced guilt of believing I had done someone an undue injustice.

And then, in the midst of all my mental and emotional distress, my grandmother died. My uncle died a week later. Then my grandfather died just a few weeks after that. Feeling very alone and really wanting someone's arms to hold me is how I ended up in "old friend's" bed. My final attempt to get his attention was to drop the panties. And of course, it worked—for the moment anyway. I gave "old friend" my panties, and in return he gave me a few moments of his time.

Now, the sexual encounter with "old friend" was an altogether different experience for me. It was the best sex I think I ever had in my life! I was undone. I was flabbergasted. I had never experienced such chemistry as I had with this man sexually. If I was confused before we had sex, I was certainly dumbfounded afterwards. Here's what you need to know: of course the sex was going to be great. We had an intimate connection already established. We had been playing with sexual fantasy for the past several months. I was trying to bait him back into my life. And when I'm at a low emotional point anyway, my normal drug of choice is large concentrated doses of MAN by injection only. All of these factors were influential to what took place in "old friend's" bed.

What God revealed to me is that the sex was great because it was orchestrated by the devil. Now this doesn't mean that every sinful sexual encounter is going to be "the best

WHERE I LEFT MY PANTIES

sex ever." But it does mean that a good tactic the enemy uses to keep many people trapped in sexual bondage is to ensure that the sinful experience is an enjoyable one. My particular sexual experience was designed to keep me wanting more—just like a drug. It was designed to keep my mind entangled in this fantasy I had constructed about me and "old friend." Maybe I'm the only woman who can attest to replaying and rehearsing the entire sex scene in homage to its greatness. And replay I did. Rehearse I did. And want more—OH YES, I did.

Even after a morning of great sex (for me at least), I was still a single woman. I still had no commitment from "old friend". And I was still reluctant to voice my desire for one as well. Again, I began the whole ordeal of anxiety, panic, and non-confrontation about the status of our acquaintance. We would be in constant communication for a few weeks, and then he would draw back for some unknown reason, leaving me feeling unsure about what was going on between us.

I had opened myself to this man on several fronts, so naturally I was garnering some expectations of him. I felt as though I needed some assurance in order to feel like I was a genuine part of his life. Because the truth of the matter is that I was not. I was still just a friend. Now, I was a friend "with benefits". I can't even say that I was totally against the idea either.

That overwhelming conviction I had years ago when I transgressed against God with some random man, I didn't have that with this man. You see, I had pretty much taken off all of my brakes.   That is, my sensitivity to the Holy Spirit had been diminished.   By ignoring the original warning signs with "old friend" when things were getting out of hand, I made it easier to walk into other acts of sin (notice I said WALK and not FALL). My spirit and my conscience were so used to being ignored that by the time I engaged in sex with this man, I literally didn't even feel convicted by it.

All I knew at that moment is that I was lonely and hurting and wanting him to be a part of my life again.   Let me clarify, I was not using sex to lure him back into my life.   I was using sex to medicate myself from life and if he decided to be a part of my life, I was not against that idea either.   Basically, I was willing to completely give myself over to the desires of my flesh if it meant that the end result would be a relationship or something close to it.

I was desperately-seeking-status.   I wanted a real relationship with this man.   I wanted a relationship PERIOD, but certainly with this man that I had known for nearly twenty years (yes you read that right-20 years).   Certainly, I wanted a relationship with this man that my heart wanted to be with.   It was sad really.   I had become the kind of woman I really didn't like.   The kind of woman who lets a man play with her emotions and pretends she's OK with it.   The kind of woman who is so lonely she would rather have a piece of a man than a whole man that desires to be with her exclusively.   I didn't like *that kind of woman* because I didn't understand what it felt like to love a man so much and want him to love you back to the degree that you put yourself in contorted positions just hoping that he will eventually take notice and come to the conclusion that you're the one he wants. I didn't understand how it felt to be lonely to the point of wanting to do anything in order to say "I got a man." I was learning something about being a single adult woman in the twenty-first century I had not known before. And I didn't like what this knowledge was turning me into.

Because I still had the remnants of some self-worth left, I again broke things off with "old friend" in an effort to redirect myself. There was something on the inside of me letting me know that what was going on between us just wasn't right (and let the church say "DUH"). I knew all the clues were there early on in this acquaintance, but I was helpless to heed them because my heart, my mind and my body were all entangled with emotions (take note of all three of those elements). Deep down, I knew I was better than the way "old friend" was treating me.

I knew I should have called him on his inability and unwillingness to make a commitment to me early on in our almost-relationship, or at least let my own desires be made known upfront. But I was afraid. I was afraid that there wouldn't be "another man like him" if I voiced my demands and he decided to take his interest elsewhere. The conflict between what I knew and felt was going on between us, versus my weak emotional status left me incapable of taking the appropriate actions to assert my self-worth. Because the truth was, my self-worth was in short supply. Having been single for about a decade with only a few dates sprinkled here and there that led nowhere, I was beginning to believe that I wasn't going to get another opportunity to be someone's significant other. However, even with my meager reserves of self-esteem, I couldn't continue feeling cast aside by "old friend." And once again, I brought our rollercoaster to a brief halt (yes you read that correctly—BRIEF, as in this ride had not come to its ultimate end yet).

I had become so unsure of myself. I was unsure about whether I should feel guilty for wanting him to make a decision about us. I was unsure about whether I had done the right thing in breaking it off...again. My mind was going 200MPH in every direction except up. I even did the whole feeling guilty for ending this non-relationship bit and apologized to him, again with no acknowledgement from him. I was seriously feeling psychotic. Truthfully, I think that going through such highs and lows with a man can engender some form of psychosis.

I don't think men really understand how we women love. I think it is worth noting that when God issues directives to husbands and wives in the book of Ephesians, he explicitly tells husbands "love your wives" (5:25). He says it again in Colossians 3:19. But He doesn't tell wives to love husbands back. Could it be that God knows that love is just what women do? Could it be that God designed us to innately, genuinely love from the very core of who we are without being prompted to do so? Not only that, but even without being the recipients of the love that we give, we still love unabashedly, unrelentingly, unyieldingly and unashamedly. WE LOVE HARD. And I believe with all that is within me, God knows that about us. So much so that he cautions men in 1 Peter 3:7 to be careful to treat us with special regard because we are the "weaker vessel." That word "weaker" in this verse does not in any way connote the chauvinistic idea that men are superior. NO—this word means delicate, gentle, priceless.

I happen to have grown up in the south. My grandmother had several curio cabinets filled with fine china and porcelain figurines. Let me tell you something about growing up in the south—as a black girl anyway. Curio cabinets, china cabinets, display cases that bear within them china and figurines of all sorts are holy grails unto black grandmothers the south over. To touch, graze, or even brush-up-against too closely to granny's china cabinet meant certain SUDDEN death.

The china was special and could not be touched with bare hands. Even the dirt and natural oils from our hands could mar the china forever. And if by chance a piece of granny's precious china would have fallen (which it never did—but for the sake of the story indulge me), it would have been impossible to piece back together again. The shards would have most likely lacerated the clean-up crew. The china would have been ruined and never put back together properly. In fact, it would have to be completely pulverized into dust and remade into something new if it were going to be used again.

That's weak china. Beautiful, precious to behold, delicate, yet extremely sharp and dangerous when broken, must be handled with the utmost care. That's china. That's women in the eyes of God but also in the hands of men.   To break a woman's heart is to break the heart of God.   That's why God tells men to be careful how they treat us.   That's why God cautions and commands men several times: "LOVE YOUR WIVES."   God knows that women thrive on affection.   He knows what the heart of a woman needs, after all, He designed it.

I know I left you with a cliff-hanger in regard to me and "old friend".   You're just going to have to read on to see where this "relationship" was finally laid to rest.

Chapter 2

It's OK to be naked

K, so I've just taken my panties off in front of you. *What's the reason for that?* You may be wondering. Glad you asked. I did that to show you it's ok to be naked. As mortifying as much of the things that I discussed in the last chapter are to me, I have a feeling that I am not the only woman in California, the United States or even the world who struggles with issues related to sex, trust and men on top of being a Christian. While the events themselves were extremely uncomfortable for me, letting it all out is somehow comforting to me. It's a reminder that I'm human and I need help that only

God can give me; and a reminder that God is the only one who covers me for real. I have to also learn not to get too comfortable while I'm clothed, because I am still subject to doing something shameful. So if I can take my panties off—quite publicly—and be real about where I am and who I am, hopefully, you will arrive at your own estimation of comfort in nakedness.

Let me tell you a story. When my girls were toddlers, every couple of days after having a bath we would have "naked time." I would let them run around the house absolutely naked for hours or until they wanted to dress themselves for bed. As a young mother of girls I just thought it was important for them to "air out". Our female bodies are uniquely, divinely designed with nooks and crannies and crevices and such. Not every place on our body gets the fresh air that it needs. So my response to this was "naked time". My girls loved it too. When I say they loved it that is a huge understatement. Mostly, I wanted them to feel comfortable in their little bodies.

I also wanted them to know that it's ok to be naked, especially in front of mommy who will never make them feel ashamed of their bodies. My girls are teenagers now, and despite my concerted effort of comfort in nakedness they are just as awkward and uncomfortable in their bodies as any teenage girl. Even so, I believe that now, at least they know that every now and then a woman's body has got to get some air in every (I DO mean every) place.

As a woman myself, I have learned that it's ok to go to bed without panties. I'm just going to say it, *My booty needs to get some air y'all...and I think yours does too.* On a deeper level, I believe there is a spiritual component to "airing-out". I think it is important as humans, not just Christians, to take everything off and stand in the open air, void of anything that would cover who we really are at that moment. I have to go back to Adam and Eve. You see, the way they fell into sin is no different than how we fall into it today.

While they were in their normal naked state, God was completely unconcerned with their nakedness. I have heard theologian after theologian say something to the effect, "they were covered by God's glory". That's a nice concept, but that is not what the bible says. The bible makes a distinct point to mention that BEFORE they sinned they were indeed naked. Bear with me here please; I'm going somewhere with this. Even after they sinned, it was not God who actually sought to cover them initially; they did that on their own. God only wanted to know where they were hiding and who told them that they were naked. I believe God was more concerned with why they felt the need to hide from HIM than anything else.

As a parent, I often see my children naked. As they are getting older, they try to hide from me. Because I was aware of their nakedness before they even knew what naked was, I see it as ridiculous for them to try and hide from me. Did you catch that? I don't think it's any different with God. He made humans in His image. For all we know, He could have been

37

naked up in heaven. The bottom line is this: God is aware of our nakedness and unmoved by it, but He still wants us to come to him in that state—naked. Unhindered. Uninhibited. What does that mean? To be naked is to be uncovered. To be uncovered is to be revealed. To be revealed is to be vulnerable. And to be vulnerable is to be real—genuine. I believe that is what God desires most of all—genuineness. Even when that genuineness seems to threaten all that we know and all that comforts us, God requires it.

I think about the woman who fell at the feet of Jesus begging for her daughter to be healed. This story takes place in the 15th chapter of the book of Matthew. In verse 22 the woman makes her appearance to Jesus. She was a Canaanite; Jews and Canaanites were not on speaking terms when Jesus walked the earth to say the absolute least. Aside from the fact that she is a female, she is also of a cultural background steeped in idol worship. But somehow she knows that Jesus is the only person who can help her. This Canaanite woman spent her life submerged in a society whose traditions scale the spectrum of such practices as temple prostitution in honor of Baal and a host of other activities that were highly offensive to the Jewish community.

She has no right to even speak to Jesus in a public place. But she does. Jesus actually ignores her at first. He doesn't say a word to her or even acknowledge her presence. When He does speak, He says, "I was sent only to the lost sheep of the house of Israel" (Matt 15:24 NASB). To this statement she falls down at his feet and worships Him. Awkward huh? Being ignored by a man brought her to her knees in worship—that's worth thinking about. But her spoken reply is merely, *"Lord, help me"* (Matt 15:24). Careful study of this passage indicates that she is actually screaming this at the top of her lungs. She was desperate.

This Canaanite woman, who had most likely only heard of Jesus and the things that He could do, left the comfort of her social status to bow herself before a Jewish man, a Jewish man who was now rejecting her openly. The story gets deeper. Jesus proceeds to liken this nameless woman to a dog. In the very next verse He states, "*It is not meet to take the children's bread and to cast it to dogs*" (15:25). Dreana's version: "I would much rather help my own kind than a dog like you." I'm just going to be blunt right now; *THAT'S COLD BLOODED!* As a woman, I can easily see myself asking a favor of someone the first time, being rejected, and then going on about my business. This woman took rejection to a whole 'nutha level. I have to bear in mind that this is a public situation.

No doubt, throngs of people are now watching the very public humiliation of this Canaanite woman begging a Jewish man for help. The woman was literally groveling at the feet of Jesus—a Jew, a man, and a person considered beneath her based on the social structure of the time period.

This Canaanite woman, who is normally admired for her tenacity, earns a deeper respect from me. You see, when Jesus

39

refused and refused and refused to acknowledge her, he was treating her the way his fellow Jewish contemporaries would have and most likely had treated her already. Not only that, she actually validates this harsh treatment herself. The final rejection by Jesus brought this woman face-to-face with some "truth." That was her exclamation—"Truth Lord." She basically said to Jesus "Yes I am a dog." Can I go a little deeper? I have to also believe that she came face-to-face with her entire lineage in this one moment.

I believe that she was forced to recall the truth about the idolatry of her culture. She was forced to consider the truth about her own lifestyle. She was forced to view the woman that she really was. She was forced to tally up the remnants of value that she thought she had accrued by being a part of the popular society to which she belonged. And when she added it all up she arrived at worthless, no more significant than a dog. "Truth Lord." That's boldness and nakedness if I have ever seen it before.

She continues to remove layers of self-righteousness as she proceeds with, *"yet the dogs eat of the crumbs which fall from their master's table"* (Matt. 15:25 emphasis mine). In this final statement she identifies Jesus as her own master. In this moment Jesus is no longer the Jewish man refusing to help her; He is also the master of her destiny and future. At this critical point of transition, the Canaanite woman leaves everything at the feet of Jesus. She took everything off in this final assertion—panties and all. And to this fearless presentation of

40

nakedness Jesus was moved to cover her. With love and mercy and even admiration, Jesus covers this Canaanite woman.

How did He do this? He endearingly gives her an identity. Then he grants her heart's truest desire. He replies, *"O woman great is your faith, let it be to you as you desire"* (Matt 15:28 NKJV emphasis mine). Jesus doesn't just call this Canaanite female a "woman" versus a dog, but He calls her a woman of "great" faith—a title that He uses very few times in scripture. I have to believe that not many a Canaanite would be ascribed such a title given the obvious differences in their religious beliefs and customs—and certainly not a Canaanite woman. Jesus gave this Gentile person a new way to identify herself. And in that moment her heart's desire was granted.

By her willingness to strip herself of societal dictates, past erroneous teachings, and the guilt that accompanied them all by acknowledging her own truth, the Canaanite woman moved Jesus to complete and utter compassion and in so doing secured her future. A person's children are directly connected to their future. Children are directly and indirectly bequeathed everything their parents instill in them both naturally and spiritually.

This woman's daughter represents her future and the shift in identification that Jesus gave her. This woman now has the responsibility of teaching her daughter a new way to live outside of their culture. Jesus had just simultaneously healed the woman's past, present and future because she was unafraid to bare it all before Him and the countless onlookers witnessing this life changing event. Nakedness must mean something to God then. But why is it so hard for us to be naked in front of Him? This is where I believe Adam and Eve can shed light on our paths.

When Adam and Eve became aware of their nakedness they undoubtedly felt guilt for the first time. And not understanding what guilt was, they tried to cover up their personal internal shamefulness by using an external remedy. Their original unconcern with their own nakedness had vanished, and it was replaced with shame. I don't believe they were actually ashamed because they were naked, but they were ashamed because they had disobeyed God and didn't know what that meant or understand the consequences of that act. What would have happened if they would have met God as they normally did and fessed up? The problem that I see going on in this original sin story is a lack of trust. For all of their meeting and talking with God on a day-to-day basis they were completely unaware and unconvinced of His love for them.

So when Adam and Eve feel the sting of guilt for the first time, an awareness of disorder had to flood them. All they had ever known up to this point was order. All they had known was God's way of doing things. The moment they stepped outside of that, they were unsure of what awaited them on the other side. This is the problem I believe many of us struggle with. We walk into a sinful situation either completely aware of what we're doing, or tempted beyond our capacity to withdraw ourselves.

And once we partake of that sinful thing, whatever it may be, we are unsure of where we now stand with God. Is He mad at us because we gave in? Is He not going to answer any more of our prayers now that we've fallen? Are we going through hell because of our disobedience? This is where I believe fear comes into play—not knowing what the consequences are. And not understanding God's character—specifically His love and His compassion for us.

Adam and Eve knew what God had said, but did they understand death? Did they know what that meant when God said it to them? They had no knowledge or understanding of disobedience. And naturally, they had no knowledge of consequences. Let me say this: I am in no way dumbing down the first family. I believe that they were incredibly intelligent, after all Adam had named, categorized and cataloged every living non-human organism.

Certainly, he was not unintelligent. But the concept of asking for forgiveness, I believe, was beyond them because they had never sinned. Even so, their inability to come before God properly didn't stop Him from showing them mercy. And even in their paralysis, they at least came to an acknowledgement of the truth. I believe that is the only reason why they were able to obtain God's mercy.

By all rights, the two of them should have just fallen dead after consuming corruption. But they did not. God had to punish them, but He did not destroy them. What is extremely

43

striking to me is that they do NOT immediately die. That fact alone is an act of God's mercy. Instead of condemning them and starting the whole creation process over again, He chooses to cover them. Instead of killing Adam and Eve, God killed an animal. He made the very first sacrifice in order to protect the lives of His creation, and He also made the very last sacrifice with Jesus.

I know you're probably weary of "A" and "E" by now, but this story shows me God's genuine character where mercy is concerned. When He has the right and the opportunity to destroy and end life, He instead chooses to protect it. How does this relate to us? I believe that God wants His children to know that He can be trusted. With our obvious guilt and shame and complete unworthiness—God can be trusted. Trusted not to kill us when our actions so rightly deserve death. Trusted to cover us instead of condemn us. Trusted to give us another chance even when we have not even asked Him for one. And trusted to secure our future.

You see, Adam and Eve never repented to God for their actions. They didn't ask God to give them a second chance. He just knew that they needed one and He graciously extended it in the form of alleviating their newfound personal discomfort in nakedness.

That particular discomfort continues to dog the trail of humanity. Just as Adam and Eve were crippled by the acute awareness of their lack of clothing, likewise many women today are rendered incapable of being completely naked before God. We want to believe that God is able to be trusted, but when we have to look at the real naked truth about ourselves, such as I just revealed in the last chapter, it's easy to have second thoughts about God's loving nature.

The Canaanite woman we discussed earlier understood this. She had to be prepared for possible rejection. She knew entirely who she really was, all that she stood for and all that people thought of her. But she took a chance on Jesus. While she was probably thinking that He was her last hope, she undoubtedly found out that Jesus was the only hope she needed. Can we be real with God like that? Can we be real about our sexual desires? Can we be real about what our hearts truly desire beyond sex? Can we be real with God about the fleeting comfort of masturbation and pornography? Can we be real with God about the real reasons we want to be married (again for many of us)? Can we come face-to-face with who we really are in front of God?

This kind of transparency is threatening and dangerous. Threatening because, once we are able to declare the truth about ourselves, the enemy can no longer torment us with it. The bible says in John 8:32 (KJV) *"And you shall know the truth and the truth shall make you free."* I believe this scripture applies to all truths, not just the truth about Jesus. For instance, if we know the truth about chocolate cake—that consuming it in large portions ad infinitum will cause us a considerable amount of caloric intake which will ultimately lead to weight gain—then we

45

are simultaneously free from the torment of "to eat or not to eat." Knowing and being fully aware of the truth about anything brings freedom.

Therefore, if we can know the truth about our ugliness and nakedness, we cannot be bound by it. If you can look in the mirror and admit that there are stretch marks in places they shouldn't be, dimples that are not on your face, or whatever might cause you to want to cover up—as unsightly as those things may be to you—the knowledge of them cannot hurt you. Such knowledge may motivate you to want to change some things about yourself.

However, all you can do when they are pointed out is say "Truth Lord." And this threatens the devil. Just like Jesus was compelled to cover the Canaanite woman, and God Himself was likewise moved to cover Adam and Eve, God will in like manner respond to our awareness of our own truth with covering grace.

This is the part that's hard to grasp; revealing our nakedness, and allowing God to cover us and believing that He will and does. In order for me to clean my body, I have to take my panties off. If I'm going to take an adequate shower, I have to be nude. The cute panties need to go. The comfortable panties need to go. The sexy panties we buy knowing we want somebody else to see them eventually, likewise, need to go. The edible panties—yes dear—those need to be disposed of too. The same natural concept applies in the spiritual world. God cannot cover us and dress us in His righteousness and grace when we attempt to make ourselves APPEAR right with externalities. Such as, the pomp-and-circumstance of church involvement, the smiles and praises we want people to believe are genuine or the "saved single and satisfied" title we don actually hoping that a certain "single brother" at the church will notice and be moved to investigate.

All of these are mere ploys to appear right or OK. At least they were for me for a period of time. While I was in my "delivered from sexual sin" state, I had a genuine resolve to flee from the appearance of all evil. But the desire to be with a man was still there. For a season that desire didn't consume me, but it was definitely still there.

But here's the punch-line, in that former delivered state, I got comfortable and prideful. And I see many a young lady in that position right now—always going on and on about "Jesus is my husband," "I don't need a man" and the ever popular "I'm single and satisfied." I will not deny that a woman can live this Christian life, be single and devoted to God without feeling the sting of loneliness. But I will temper that declaration with this: *"So if you think you are standing firm, be careful that you don't fall!"* (1 Corinthians 10:12 NIV). Been there, done that, got the heart scars to prove it—and as a matter of fact, you just read about it.

Being naked with God means that we are willing to admit that we would like to be in a relationship with an actual flesh-and-blood man. Acknowledging this as truth is freeing;

47

and it's OK. The only thing God said was NOT good was for man (meaning HUMANS) to be alone. So if God says it's NOT OK to be alone, why is there such a massive push in this society to force women to be OK in that state?

Happily married women are quick to tell single women, "you don't *need* a man," "be *grateful* for your singleness," and even, "don't let a man *validate* you." I absolutely understand the ideology behind all of these mantras, and I even agree to an extent. But if God says it's not good for me to be alone why should I feel good about it? I just don't believe that God is sin support of *people* being alone. Our God is relational by His very own design; God in three distinct manifestations (Father, Son and Holy Spirit) simultaneously working individually yet beautifully in unity. And still we tell single women to enjoy their single status. Enjoy their loneliness. Enjoy their isolation. I just can't agree that God wants me to enjoy being alone when HE HIMSELF said it is NOT good.

We have been conditioned in this society to accept what is the norm against what is God's design. We actually create an alternate truth to satisfy what our present conditions are. Because there are thousands of single women waiting to be found by a husband, and no real explanation for this phenomenon can be offered, we tell them, "Oh you don't need a man anyway." When the truth is that they do. It is not God's design for mothers to raise children alone, nor fathers. We tell men to look for perfect women, not the hurting imperfect women that make up the majority. God told husbands to love their wives as

Christ loves the church (Ephesians 5:25). Well, I haven't found a perfect church yet. I haven't found a church without faults and flaws and unsightly scars and wounds. Yet, many men in this society are being told in churches to run away from women who "are not whole." I see hypocrisy in that.

I am not saying that we all shouldn't be striving and reaching toward wholeness in Christ. We absolutely should be doing our best to be our best selves whether we are in a romantic relationship or not. However, loving as Christ loves equals loving others with the knowledge of their imperfections, flaws, BAGGAGE and wounds. Christ loves YOU and ME with our imperfections. So how can we tell people not to do the same in relationships that are romantic or otherwise?

For every woman who can sincerely profess to living without loneliness and having no desire for the companionship of a man, I applaud you. But I urge you to guard your heart. Deal gently with US women who struggle in our singleness. And don't pass judgment on US. Pray for US, respect US and show US love, mercy and compassion. That's what Jesus does. Singleness in the twenty-first century is NOT a joke. Women have been wounded by man after man after man without reprieve. And then she has to go to church and feel isolated and cast aside while preachers and evangelists condemn her for being "easy," "loose," "not whole." When the real truth is that her heart is broken and she needs to feel loved, accepted, approved, and affirmed. These last necessities are not going around churches or the world at lightning speed. Wounded women are in hiding—some "hiding in the open." Too afraid to come out and say as LL Cool J, an 80s rapper, once said "I NEED LOVE!" And YES every human NEEDS love.

I can speak so candidly about my Christian singleness because that's where I've been and that's where I am now. I've been that Christian woman who was in church three-to-four days a week, children in tow, shouting "Hallelujah!" on the first row. I was not faking the funk. But I was in silent torment. Loneliness, confusion and frustration were eating me alive. For all of my trying to look good and make everyone think that I was OK, the real truth is that I was suffering silently. My heart crumbled a little every time I would see couples walking into church hand-in-hand smiling, like life was so great.

Preachers addressing "husbands of the church" or "wives of the church" with smiles as if laughing to some inside joke single people were not privy to. Jealous and hurt, I wore the "comfortable" panties of church involvement and busied myself senseless until my children were not being sufficiently taken care of at home. I spent my nights lonely and afraid. Afraid of what anyone would think of me if they knew how very badly I really wanted to give my panties to another man. Not because I simply like giving my panties away, but because I want to be received. I want to be held. I want to be sexy for some man that will have me. I want to be loved by a man. I want to have sex again—legally. And these desires are not sins or sinful.

I mentioned earlier that there is a confidence in knowing that a man finds you attractive. That boils down to the need to be accepted that all humans have. But women seem to carry this need a little closer to their hearts. We need to know that we matter to someone. We need to know that we are not invisible. We need to know that we are loved by someone—and our children (for those who are blessed with them) are not enough.

When these very specific needs go unmet, we will find an outlet or *in*let to meet them ourselves. This is one major reason why I am particularly so fond of sex. In an instant, I am received, accepted, needed—I matter to the man involved in a sexual act with me (and in many cases I pretend that I matter). For those few seconds, I am special. The problem with using sex to meet any or all of these innate needs is that sex can only meet them intermittently and sporadically. I will eventually need to have another sexual encounter to obtain this temporary and artificial satisfaction.

And when a flesh-and-blood penis is unavailable, many of us will settle for a synthetic replica, or our own hands—enter masturbation. The comfort of this act is that it provides that sexual stimulation without the extra guilt of "really" fornicating with a man (and don't get it twisted, there is still a level of guilt involved). But on a more serious note, masturbation or outright sex provides a form of affection. Sex is probably the most intimate act of affection. All at once, you are giving and receiving. And science has already proven the sedation inducing powers of an orgasm, so sex is also a means of relaxation. In the act of sex there is equal exchange of affection coupled with comfort—two of the most important ingredients of a woman's need base. Yet we still wonder why some women are so quick to open their legs to men that merely pay them a compliment.

The truth? In a twisted sort of way she's actually opening her heart in an attempt to receive affection. That's the real missing ingredient in the lives of many women who engage in masturbation or fornication with a man or even another woman (we might as well recognize that homosexuality exists—though I do not support it). Affection seeking is the real issue.

This is why the needs of women need to be met by someone who can meet them completely and perpetually. Only Jesus can provide this kind of love and satisfaction. But we must be willing to give Him the opportunity. I think about the woman at the well and how many men must have had a pair of her panties. You will find this story in chapter 4 of the book of John. I believe in my heart that when she saw Jesus, without knowing Who He was, she was thinking of giving her panties to Him too. She was at a well, THEE well. The same well she went to day after day to draw water from. When Jesus began to speak to her, she mentioned how deep the well was and that Jesus had nothing to draw water with. I don't think she was talking about the well particularly. I believe she was talking about the hole in her soul. How deep that hole runs in the heart of a woman who has been disappointed. How deep that hole runs in the heart of a woman who has been let down by men, other women, family and friends that claimed to love her.

That hole can run especially deep when a woman has been hurt by the church. Hurt by the people of God that she trusted to help her and love her and be a place of safety to her. This nameless woman thought that Jesus didn't have the right instrumentation to draw out of her the deep wounds of her soul. But the bible says in Psalm 42:7 that *"deep calls unto deep,"* so when Jesus asked her about her husband, he proved he indeed had the right instrument to draw with.

That one question unlocked for this woman, years, I imagine, of pain and heartache and un-dealt with sorrow. On being asked of her husband, she was forced into pulling out her panties. She quickly made a pass at Jesus, as far as I'm concerned. I know how easy it is to revert to my usual self-preservationist way of handling things when I feel pressured to perform. I know how it feels to try and divert the attention away from me to something else that puts me back in control of the situation. "I don't have a husband," she replied.

I can imagine her being flushed at first. Then, thinking quickly—because women know how to think on their feet— she moves in for the kill. She arrives at the solution to seduce this handsome young man that was seated before her. Seduce him because it was more comfortable to use her body to control him, than deal with the truth of how she really felt. Seduce him because she knows no other way of relating to a man than relinquishing her panties to one in hopes that she will be received by him. Deep down, I believe she wanted a husband. I believe she was tired of men partaking of her body and leaving her well damn-near empty.

When I consider the men I gave so many of my panties to, I am left feeling guilty and ashamed of myself. Guilty because, I am a Christian woman trying to live my life in a way that truly pleases God. Ashamed because, the route of escape may very well be outlined but my body refuses to take it most of the time. Paul said it best, "the good I want to do, I just can't do it. But the evil I would rather not do, I can't stop doing that" (Rom 7:19 paraphrased). As Christians we hold this verse up seemingly as a license to excuse our sinful behavior in many cases. But the truth is that sin is hard to stop. It is literally our human nature to engage in sin. It feels good—shoot—it feels great. Otherwise it wouldn't be so tempting.

Personally, I am a woman who enjoys having sex. There, I said it (as if you hadn't figured that one out by now). Having been married for a few years I had grown accustomed to expecting sex on a regular basis. It was a comfort to me. My body had grown used to it. I think the same can be said of women in relationships that mimic marriage—long term "shacking up." The bottom line is that once you get used to having sex it is difficult to suddenly not be able to engage in it any longer. Your body misses it. Your mind misses it. Your heart misses it. In many cases, you may not necessarily miss the person you had sex with that you may have divorced or are no longer in a relationship with. But sex itself becomes a missed friend.

Being deprived of the comfort of regular sex that you've grown accustomed to having is like being told not to eat or breathe until you get married. Physically, emotionally and psychologically, I believe, you go through withdrawals. Let me just speak for myself right now—I went through withdrawals. And to be quite honest (here I go again with the taking off of my panties) I still go through withdrawals.

I don't know what God did when He created sex, but there is something unique about it that, once you have started having it, the off button is hard to find. I'm sure God designed it this way on purpose in order to bless marriages. Yet, once you have had sex outside of marriage, the absence of it is tormenting. Outside of marriage, sex can also be the most hurtful form of manipulation ever known. Sex outside of marriage is not honored or respected by God for the blessing He intended it to be. God's greatest design for sex is that it be enjoyed between a husband and a wife. When these parameters are not met, sex is detrimental to spiritual health, emotional health and psychological health.

Even so, knowing the tormenting effects of sinful sex doesn't prevent every unmarried person from engaging in it. And I believe the reasons behind that truth lie in the fact that every person desires and needs attention, affection, affirmation, approval and acceptance. These five elements comprise the avenues through which every human recognizes that they are LOVED. It all comes down to the fact that every person desires and needs LOVE. People are willing to meet these basic human needs in ways that compromise their Christianity, their personal security and their better judgment. One main reason for this is because few people are willing to truly LOVE others in the sacrificial way that Jesus does.

God knows that, and I believe He understands that better than we give Him credit for. God is not some autonomous despot unwilling to relate to us. My point is that God does not sit in heaven looking down on His children in disappointment when they fall into habitual sin. I believe He hates it. But I also believe He is more hurt by the knowledge of what sin does to us than the fact that we sin. He is hurt when sin keeps us from coming to Him.

When we take the fig leaves of guilt and try to cover our sin with smiles and seeming humility instead of being naked before a Father Who will never make us feel ashamed, God is hurt the most. Because God understands our need for affection, affirmation, approval, attention, acceptance and love, He willingly desires to meet all of those needs Himself. But we have to be willing to allow God to change our minds about what love is. And we must be willing to behold our own personal truth—nakedness.

God's ultimate desire for us is that we know that He loves us. God's love for us looks differently than what we have grown accustomed to considering love. God's love for us moved Him to send Jesus to the earth and die for us. God's love for us keeps Him always coming back to us when we mess things up—in fact, He never leaves us when we think He has. God's love is not something we earn.

And it is certainly not something that we can do anything to deserve. Jesus is the ultimate representation of God's love for us. Acknowledging Jesus is all at once acknowledging God's love and admitting our need for Him. This may sound simple, but it's not an easy concept to grasp when you feel dirty. It's not easy to do when you feel like your panties are on display for the whole world to see. That woman at the well knew about having her panties on display. That's why she went to the well when no one else was there.

She didn't want to see the other women of the city, because they probably knew all of her business too. Business that she didn't care to be confronted with everyday everywhere she went. The whispers, the sharp looks. While every other woman in town was drawing water near sunset, she was drawing hers in the middle of the day—the hottest part of the day. She would rather suffer the heat of the sun beading down on her while she lugged heavy pitchers full of water back to her home than endure the shame and criticism of fellow women. She was hiding out in the open—or so she thought. But Jesus came looking for her; to meet her on her own terms, on her own turf.

Jesus found her.   Just like God found Adam and Eve while they thought that they were hiding from Him.   God looked for them. He sought them out and met them on their own terms—clad in inadequate fig leaves.

How do we arrive at the concept of agreeing that God is the One who can meet all of our human needs?   How do we believe that God can be trusted with our nakedness?   We bare it all in front Him by faith.   We admit that we have some unsightly ugliness that we are not proud of.   And we do this on our own terms.   I can't give you a formula for finding out for yourself that God can be trusted with your nakedness.   You have to discover this on your own.   It's going to be unnatural at first and certainly uncomfortable.   But it is necessary if you want to learn a facet of God's character that you've never known before.

To me, being naked looks like this: "God you made me to desire a man sexually.   I know that that desire should be reserved for the man you have set apart for me to marry.   While my heart truly wants to wait for that man Lord, doggone it my panties are on fire right about now!!   Help me please!"   In that acknowledgement there is utter nudity.

But what happens when this particular woman heeds the desire of her flesh rather than the beckoning of her Father to abstain?   Is she now cast off as a sinful harlot who had better not dare step foot inside of a church?   Should she be esteemed lower than her sisters who don't struggle with sexual desire as she does?   Or those sisters whose fig leaves may be a bit broader than her own—those who can camouflage themselves and pretend that they have no struggles?

Absolutely not!   While I know that God is able to grant some women reprieve of sexual desire, after all, I experienced it myself, I also know that other women do not have the capacity to abstain from sex completely.   Not just the capacity, but also the support and genuine love from a closely knit group of people in order to sustain abstinence.   This is not me trying to take hope away from women who want to live an abstinent life.   This is me being very blunt about the topic of sex.

Every woman is not going to wait for Boaz to find her before she engages in sexual activity.   We should absolutely warn her of the emotional and spiritual dangers of sex outside of marriage.   But even if she cannot wait, it is cruel and unfair to make her feel cast off and thrown away and unfit for the kingdom of God.   That's not how God deals with people. God woos people with love.   God is able to comfort and continue loving a woman even through her mess.

I think about the story of Mephibosheth, which takes place in the 9th chapter of 2nd Samuel.   He was the son of Jonathon, who was the best friend of King David, and the grandson of King Saul.   Mephibosheth had been crippled at a young age, having been dropped by his nurse (2Samuel 4:4). Once Jonathon died, King David wanted to show his appreciation to someone in Jonathon's family for the friendship he had enjoyed with him. The friendship between David and Jonathon is very unique and important to our study of relationships today.

I'll revisit this topic later on in the following chapters. When David found Mephibosheth, he restored his rightful place in the kingdom as an heir of the former king—King Saul (Jonathon's dad). David went as far as to let the crippled man sit at the feasting table with him—the king. The man, who was too crippled to help himself, found favor with the king to the degree that the king appointed others to assist him. And in his incapacitated state, he was seated at the king's table enjoying every benefit of those who were not so inhibited.

To me, this means that there will be some women who may always struggle with a sinful habit such as sex outside of the covenant of marriage, but God has appointed others to assist her and continue loving her as though she had no sinful struggle. Not a popular argument. I'm aware of that.

The bible says this: *"Dear brothers and sisters, if another believer is overcome by some sin, you who are godly should gently and humbly help that person onto the right path. And be careful not to fall into the same temptation yourself"* (Gal 6:1 NLT). The very next verse goes on to say, *"Carry each other's burdens, and in this way you will fulfill the law of Christ."* And what is the law of Christ? In John chapter 13, verse 34, Jesus tells the disciples, *"So now I'm giving you a new commandment: Love each other. Just as I have loved you, you should love each other"* (NLT). Since these are the words of Jesus, I have to conclude that these words must be the law of Christ—LOVE.

We cannot turn a deaf ear to the cries of women who are in need of comfort. Rejection from men hurts like nothing else I have ever known. It is this particular woundedness that plagues women and keeps them from enjoying the love of a Father—the love of God. Because so many well-meaning Christians truly do not understand God's love enough to walk in it themselves, hurting, scared, lonely women remain clothed in fig leaves incapable of trusting the God who seeks only to prove His love to them.

It is my firm belief that when a woman understands how much God truly, sincerely and completely loves her, she will no longer have a desire to break His heart with sinful activity. But a woman cannot know God's love if there is no one willing to show her what it looks like. So is it really OK to be naked? Indeed, it is. If it's just you and God—ONLY—I encourage you to take it all off girl! If there is no one to encourage you in your nakedness, or encourage you in your struggle—GOD IS NOT ASHAMED OF YOU!! Be naked in front of Him and learn for yourself the blessing of covering grace.

Chapter 3

*You can't take your panties
off for everybody*

*I*f it's OK to be naked, then who is it OK to be naked for? That's a good question. As a parent I had to learn the limits of my nakedness with my children. When they were babies, they had no clue about mommy's body, or their own for that matter. Therefore, I was very comfortable in being naked in front of them. But as they got older they became more inquisitive about certain body parts; their own as well as mine. This led me to curtail my nudeness in their presence.

In order to teach my daughters appropriateness and respect of their own bodies, it became necessary for me to model appropriateness in front of them. I learned that I couldn't just walk around the house with no panties on; I had to show them respect as well as show them that I respected myself. In doing this, I was teaching them to respect themselves and others. This principle holds firm relationally, spiritually and emotionally as well.

With that being said, it is not OK to spew nakedness around in sects where no one has qualified for the privilege of beholding utter nudity—vulnerability. *What does that mean?* It means that certain parameters of trust must be forged before individual transparency can be presented. Let me tell you another story (go ahead and get used to my stories—they run throughout this book). A few years ago I met a lady whose personality instantly drew me to her. Right away we just clicked.

Since I had previously experienced a traumatic friendship that resulted in the complete severing of the relationship, I was very cautious about engaging this new would-be friend. We began to chit-chat together at church, which led to several impromptu after church meetings over lunch. One summer she invited me and my family over to her house for the Fourth of July. I had no plans of my own, so we joined her. We began to cook together and share stories of growing up, spiritual awakenings, scriptural revelations; we just began to really talk on a deeper level. I found myself literally telling my life-story to this near stranger of a woman. But there was an ease and a comfort in doing so that I hadn't felt from many people I have crossed paths with—especially other women (this will make sense to you a little later).

As we continued to talk the day—and night—away, I watched as this woman sat before me literally stunned to the point of speechlessness from the intricate details of my life that I had divulged to her. I got naked in front of her on an emotional and relational level. In doing this I freed her to, likewise, bare herself in front of me and share her own story. We exchanged nakedness that day into the early morning hours of the next day. There was an atmosphere of mutual trust, expectation and equal exchange.

I gave a little of me; she gave a little of her. Sounds a lot like sex huh? That's because genuine transparency between people is just that intimate—especially for women who naturally simultaneously desire to give and to be received. And it is the unique mixture of these two desires that leads a lot of women into deep relationships with one another. The point I'm trying to make is that a trust had been developed between me and my friend over a period of time, to the degree that when genuine transparency was presented there was no threat of harm on either of our parts. I felt free enough to strip myself of all masks and cover-ups in front of a friend.

At the end of our deep conversation both her and my

65

children were already asleep, so we stayed the night over. But my friend did something I was not expecting; she offered me a fresh new pair of panties. Intuitively knowing that I was unprepared for a sleep-over, my friend was prepared to cover my nakedness.

How did that happen? She had proven herself able to be trusted with my nakedness. Through carefree conversation, genuine interest in who I am as a person, and the willingness and readiness to listen without judgment or harsh criticism, my acquaintance had become my friend and eventually my battle-tested sister. And this didn't happen over a long period of time; this didn't take years. It did, however, take consistency and mutual willingness to relate to one another. She was interested in knowing me for real. And I was likewise interested in knowing her. In addition, I wanted to be known by someone like me. I wanted to know that there was someone I could relate to who shared similar struggles with me.

My friend is married and has adult children, but she knows the struggles of single parenthood as well as the struggles of sexual desire. This fact gave her credibility with me. God provided an opportunity for us to share our experiences openly with one another, and my friend and I did the work of relating. This isn't happening much in the world today. And even less in churches. People are too consumed with their own lives and issues to engage someone else in an intimate relationship. And I'm not even talking about romantic relationships; I'm talking about genuine friendship development and cultivation.

You might be wondering, what does friendship—especially the homogenous type—has to do with taking your panties off for the wrong man? It has a lot more to do with it than you know. This particular friendship that God allowed me to develop is significant because I was able to openly share my goings on between me and "old friend" with my sister-friend. She listened to my gripes and complaints, my cries and my screams and never once caused shame to be birthed within me. She never made me feel less-than. She prayed for me and with me.

It's relationships of this dynamic that I know would benefit single women toughing out their singleness and sex struggles. We need to be able to share our sexual struggles, relationship struggles, or general life struggles with other women who will not beat us over the head with scriptures. Women who will not preach at us when we WALK INTO SIN eyes wide open, or fall into it nearly blind. Women who will not in turn be judgmental toward us and treat us differently now that they know particular "naked" truths about us, but will allow us to take our panties off without the threat of shame or judgment.

The bible says that we should confess our faults one to another so that the prayer of faith will heal us (James 5:16). It would be foolish of me to take my foot ailments to a gynecologist. There is an entire separate practice of medicine devoted to the health of the feet. In like manner, I can't take my single-woman issues to someone who has no knowledge of what it is to be single—right now in the twenty-first century.

Every single woman arrived at her state of singleness by different and unique means. Every struggle a single woman faces is unique to her. That doesn't mean that women of dissimilar circumstances cannot relate to one another. But it does mean that single women need a group of qualified women ready to listen and discuss their issues and offer wisdom and comfort instead of criticism and coldness. My friend had no idea that I would be spending the night at her house, but she was prepared for that event. She offered a covering—not just physically, but emotionally as well. As I shared my experiences with her, she cried with me. She wasn't quick to offer a Christian slogan. Rather, she allowed me space to just be. And that alone was a comfort to me.

In contrast, I had to learn the hard way that, oftentimes once people know some ugly truth about you, they are subject to use it against you or at least make you feel very ashamed of yourself and your struggles. At the church that I was attending during my first go-round with "old friend," I had developed a small friendship with one of the pastors. He, his wife and I would occasionally hang out apart from church functions. When I was feeling especially down I would ask him or his wife to pray for and with me. We were friends but not extremely close friends.

I had a definite check in my spirit that getting too close to this person and their family was not a good idea. This came to me out of basic interaction with this person—working with them in ministry. Watching their responses and reactions to certain life issues—nothing jaw-dropping or super spiritual either—just purposeful study of people. In any case, I knew that God was giving me an awareness of them in order to caution me about getting too close to them. And that's an OK awareness to have. I am certain that God does not want us to be paranoid about relating to people, but he certainly wants us to guard our hearts.

At the very least, however, I felt that prayer is always beneficial, no matter who it comes from (but even in this it is important to be discernful). Sounds simple, right? Well I had an issue I wanted to share with this pastor so that he could pray with me about it. Something I had been struggling with as a single parent—completely unrelated to sex or men. So I shared my issue with him. He responded to my vulnerability by asking, "Are you even saved?" I can't tell you how much that hurt me.

I had devoted so much of my time to assisting him in ministry and building a relationship with his family. Not for any other reason than to help support the work of God through ministry at my church. Yet, here he was calling me unsaved because I needed help in an area of my life (again, this issue was about my parenting skills and had nothing at all to do with anything else—I was still in "delivered" state at this time). My act of nakedness prompted scrutiny and mistrust in him. A lesson learned.

Because this minor revelation of my nakedness to this pastor-friend of mine resulted in a feeling of shame rising within me, he ultimately disqualified himself for any further attempts at an intimate friendship with me.   And to be completely honest, I don't think it is proper or in order for me—a single woman—to have an intimate personal friendship with a married man anyway.   To be clear, there was no attraction on my part or his part.   I hold the belief that women should counsel women and men should counsel men.   Heterosocial friendships that arise out of church involvement can be very dangerous when they are entered into without wisdom, especially those between single women and married men, or married women and single men. My personal bent is to not befriend married men unless their wives are friends of mine as well.   I can be friends with the couple (as was the case in this situation), but to have a friendship with a married man at church—even if said man is a pastor—is a bit out of order for me.   Just thought I'd throw this in here for good measure.

Now to continue with my issue about my pastor-friend: His unwillingness to receive my transparency as an issue he could have agreed with me in prayer over did not cause me to treat him any differently than with the respect his position warranted.   He was still pastor to me.   But from that point on I was no longer willing to venture into depths of relating to him on any other level because he made me feel ashamed versus comfortable in my nakedness.

Not comfortable in my sin issue (which this issue really was not some sinfulness on my part-rather a personal struggle). But comfortable in knowing I can share my struggle with him and not be made to feel guilty because I have something that I am struggling with. There is a difference between comfort in nakedness before people, and shamefulness brought on by people—a difference between conviction and condemnation.

I seek to be very clear about who is worthy of your nakedness. Not just your naked body, but your naked emotions, your naked spirit and your naked heart. Not everybody can handle raw nakedness appropriately. And mishandled nakedness leads to a distrust of all nakedness and a distrust of all people. When a person has been wounded by way of sharing nakedness with someone, they become very cautious and outright afraid of ever revealing themselves in that way again. That's what happened to me. But I have grown since then. That one pastor was merely my seasonal relationship disappointment.

I've been wounded in the area of friendships before him and certainly I will be again. The point of having gone through this is that I had to learn how to take cues from people and discern for myself their readiness and worthiness of me and all my stuff—with or without panties. Pastor so-and-so should have been kept within a certain partition of the intimacy hierarchy by me. And because I did not heed the cues that I knew God was giving me about delving into transparency with this person, I ended up with a label, a wounded heart and a burden of shame. It is my endeavor to help you avoid such

71

hard lessons.

People must qualify themselves in order to behold your nakedness in all of its genuine beauty.   They do this by being transparent with you and by not making you feel ashamed when you are transparent with them.   So how do we judge or discern who is worthy of our nakedness?   If you don't have Jesus then you don't have The Holy Spirit.   And without The Holy Spirit you don't have any real discernment or ability to assess a person's character.   You may think you're a good judge of character but apart from God, you can't do a thing—and that includes judge character accurately and appropriately. Shoot—even super Christians who have been saved most of their lives may still misjudge someone's character; I sure did (not that I'm a super Christian—but I think you get the point I'm making). I will say that with Jesus there will always be clues and it is up to you to heed those or not.   But without Jesus, you're on your own attempting to figure someone out.   You may as well look for a marked speck of sand in a sandbox with the lights off.

Sounds funny, but it's the truth.   I know that God can urge us and prompt us when we are on the right track, or deter us from the wrong one.   He can and will allow a person's true character to be shown.   Then, however, He leaves the decision to act on this information up to us.   He is able to lead us into worthwhile fruitful relationships with people, but still, there is a part we have to play in order to further those relationships.

God will provide the opportunities, but, just like me and my dear friend, the work of relating is up to us. And relating with people, not just men, is paramount to our Christian lives as well as our normal day-to-day lives. God did not create us to be isolated from one another. He didn't make Adam and Eve and then put Eve on the far side of the garden and tell them to get themselves together before they come together. He set Eve down right in front of Adam; He created an opportunity for them to meet and engage one another and thereby begin to cultivate a relationship. I think it's no different today. God sets up opportunities for us individuals to encounter one another and begin to cultivate relationships with each other. Because the truth is that people—Christian or not—need shoulders to lean on every now and then, arms to wrap them up in hugs once in a while, and hands outstretched ready to lift them out of a PIT-FALL.

That's what my sister-friend did for me. She prayed me out of a pit and helped to soften my fall. I needed someone strong enough, willing enough and completely nonjudgmental enough to carry me through the acute agony of heartbrokenness. What I needed most, when my heart was broken and my hopes were deferred, was someone who could relate to my tears and frustration and not ever make me feel ashamed for having those feelings.

I needed someone who would not heap shame upon me for having had the traumatic experience of giving my panties to an unqualified recipient. My sister would not even allow me to make myself feel ashamed. She comforted me and held me up in prayer when I was too weak to pray for myself. She listened intently and didn't offer criticism to my ugly, unsavory and shameful nakedness.

Alright, I guess I'll expose a bit more of that particular shameful nakedness now and finish the story of me and "old friend." We had ceased communicating with one another; well, he had ceased communicating with me. I was in a big several months long funk because I seriously felt guilty about the whole ordeal. But as time progressed, I began to realize that God was healing my wounded emotions. I began to creep, ever so slowly back to Jesus. I was slowly being restored to my "single and satisfied" state of mind. I ended up changing churches after five years at my former church. The whole event of me and "old friend" occurred during my last few months at the church.

Let me interject a thought right here: I am not a church-hopper by any means (one who continually changes churches). There was nothing particularly foul that happened at this church that caused me to leave out of offense. In fact, the many offensive things that DID happen to me, God walked me through them, and taught me some immense lessons about "church folk," myself, and Him. Trust me when I tell you, I had many opportunities to leave this church prior to the time that I did leave.

Before I left, I prayed long and hard about the decision and made sure that I had heard from God alone. Not my emotions, not other people and not out of strife or anything negative on my part—my season had just come to an end there. And the funny thing is that I had finally developed some fruitful relationships with people there. And at a low point in my life this church actually came swiftly to my aid. Even so, God told me that my time was up there and I had to move on.

My heart still hurt on account of "old friend," but I began to view the situation with this man and me in a different way. God had to take me through such an ordeal with a man in order to reveal to me the areas of my life that still needed His touch. He had to show me the things that were in my heart that I had no clue were there at all. Things like people-pleasing and low self-esteem to name just a few. In bits and pieces I was coming back together. I began hearing God again.

I had found a new church home and was getting involved again. And then, naturally, "old friend" decided to resurface. He reached out to me and even though I was hesitant at first, I reached back. Because I was not completely healed from our last ordeal, I was still very unsure of myself and insecure. True to insecure form, I desired to prove my worthiness to him. We started to converse again and get close to one another all over again. And so it began again—the love chase.

"Old friend" and I began to open up a little more about ourselves. We got a few inches deeper into each other's mental and emotional space. I was hopeful, yet again, that this time would be different. Though I was cautious about the instability of our "relationship," I still wanted to show him that I was *not* desperate and needy. I wanted to show him that if he didn't want to talk to me on a regular basis, that was OK with me. Because, in my insecure mind, I thought he was worth it. I thought he was worth me waiting by the phone for his calls. I thought he was giving me a second chance, and I didn't want to mess it up this time (sucking your teeth and shaking your head yet?). I gave him so much power over me. He was oblivious to this, of course—then again, now that I've had time to think about it, maybe he wasn't as ignorant as I supposed. I found myself going out of my way with grand gestures toward this man; I was the gallant one pursuing him—he, a mere fixture to my displays of affection toward him.

Again I began to compromise what my heart knew was right in exchange for an inkling of attention from a man. Again I began to entertain sexy conversations, this time they were even illustrated as I became a cell-phone centerfold (I told you the rollercoaster hadn't stopped). I'm sure you're thinking, "What in the HELL is wrong with you?!" Loneliness. Affectionless. Woundedness. And an acute desire to be received by some man while I still have a few good years left—maybe not all in that particular order, but definitely a whole lot of each one.

Even as I was tip-toeing back to Jesus, my heart was still connected to this guy. My heart was still a little bruised by him as well, but the bruises were eclipsed by my insatiable *desire* to be with him in some kind of way. I was willing to overlook his callousness toward me from our initial ordeal, as well as his obvious repeat behavior, in order to pretend *again* that we had something we didn't really have—a genuine relationship. Loneliness and insecurity are a terrible combination (as if I haven't made *that* point blatantly clear enough yet).

Again, he began to pull away from me. This time I attempted to at least verbalize my concern to him. It was glazed over casually and we proceeded with our pseudo-relationship. Within a few months our conversations were minimized to drive-by type "check-ups." "Just called to check on you—alright talk to you later—bye." That was a literal conversation. Nothing more than that; and that would be the conversation after several days of no contact. Contact that, for the most part, I was initiating. There was no depth, no connection, no—anything. And, again I was confused by his actions.

Things would seem to be moving along OK, and then for some reason or another he would go into stealth mode on me. Worried that I was losing him *again*, I planned a trip to visit him. My intentions were to seriously discuss the direction of whatever we were doing. We hadn't spoken in two weeks before my visit. My calls were unreturned, my texts were unanswered, so I didn't really know what to expect. And yes he knew that I was coming to visit—it was not a surprise. I just wanted to spend some time with him, reconnect and get some answers.

Needless to say, none of that happened. I take that back—all of it happened, just not to my particular liking. There was an awkwardness and distance between us that extended farther than the miles that I flew to visit him (which was literally across the country by the way). There was no feeling of excitement to see me whatsoever. And this immediately caused uneasiness and insecurity to rise within me. Adamant about wanting to enjoy my visit with him, I opted not to discuss our arrangement. For a week-long visit I spent three days with him—and just a few hours in each of those days. No real conversation. No interest. I was hurt and confused. . . again. But in true insecure form, none of that was enough to keep my legs closed. Of course I gave "old friend" the panties. . . **AGAIN**. Anxious to recapture our initial sexual experience in an effort to create some artificial similitude of a connection between us, I sidelined his suspicious behavior and tried to regain his attention by using my sexual prowess. However, this gesture proved to be, as my teenage daughters often say, an "Epic Fail."

NOTE: My hope is that you not perceive this story as me glorifying my sinful sexual experiences. That's not what I'm trying to do. My aim is to deconstruct these incidents and learn from them myself, and hopefully allow someone else to learn from them as well.

Because my mind was so wrapped up in what was not going on between us, the great sex that we are known to have was, likewise, not going on between us. But here is where the

78

line in the sand was drawn for me. I am normally a very sexually confident woman. I have never had a bad day, so to speak. I have never NOT satisfied a man sexually (yes that's a double negative from a soon-to-be English teacher—that's how serious this was to me). I hadn't dealt with a disappointed client before—like, EVER. When every other attempt at getting a man's attention would fail, I could always rely on my body to do the talking. And I would regain the upper-hand every time. Sounds like pride, I'm sure, but I promise you it's actually insecurity. So here I was with this man who had been avoiding me for weeks, had already broken my heart twice (well, two times that you all are aware of anyway), and when it's my time to shine he is not the least bit moved, if you can catch my meaning. Was I trying too hard? Was I not trying hard enough? Had I lost my touch? All I knew was that nothing was going on between the sheets like it used to. Talk about embarrassment. Talk about shame. And talk about humiliation.

That earth-quaking, mountain moving sex that we had had before was not in the building. There was a complete lack of chemistry between us this time around. Let me tell you this: whatever spiritual gifts you have been given from God do not turn off simply because you are wrapped up in sin. I know that I have the gift of discernment; that gift doesn't go away because I'm in the bed with a man that I'm not married to. Hence, I could clearly discern this man's lack of sexual interest with me while we were engaged in the act (and yes, I could discern his overall lack of interest in me as well).

And getting very real now (as if you're gonna expect less than that from me now), I believe any woman can decipher a man's sexual cues. It doesn't take the gift of discernment to tell you when a man's not feeling you in the bed. And it was one of the worst feelings I have ever known. Knowing that I'm not satisfying a man when I simultaneously know that I most certainly, unquestionably, and most definitely CAN is a heart wrenching truth to face. And I was wounded in a way that I had never been wounded by a man before in my life. Sexual rejection is one of the most hurtful forms of rejection a woman can experience.

For all of my confidence and skill in the area of sex, I managed to fall short with "old friend." But of course I can't take all the credit now can I? It does take two to tango—especially when we're talking about the horizontal tango. Neither of us was there and present in that moment. Aside from the obvious fact that it was an act of sin which neither of us should have been engaged in anyway; there are other factors that are necessary to consider.

I was absent due to mental fixation on his non communication and obvious waning interest in me. I don't really know why he was absent—I do have a few good hunches—but that's neither here nor there. The fact of the matter is that he was indeed absent. Knowing that fact only pushed me further into my mind and away from the event. I remember that initial awkward feeling of guilt and embarrassment that flooded my entire being after realizing that this sexual experience was swiftly going south. I felt so dirty and used.

You may be thinking, "How are you gonna feel used when you consented and he didn't force you to have sex with him?" There's a funny thing about being a woman when it comes to sex and affection. Because we thrive on affection, when there are genuine acts of affection shown to a woman prior to having sex, the sex is normally great for both parties. Better yet, the woman is more likely to make a concerted effort to sexually satisfy the person who has shown affection to her. Yet, when there is no affection shown to a woman, and sex proceeds regardless, commonly, women feel degraded and almost sexually assaulted. I won't say that this is a rule because there are some women who can treat sex the same way as many men treat sex—without an emotional connection.

I know this because I was such a woman. But once your emotions are engaged with someone, the sex you have with that person changes completely from a mere act to an act of affection. And this is where the danger lies. This is one main reason why sex is reserved for the marriage bed. It is a way for spouses to show affection to one another on the most personal level. Sex as an act of affection can be the most beautiful experience ever known. But when that act of affection goes unreciprocated, it can be the most emotionally damaging experience to a woman. Better yet, when one party is treating sex as an act of affection while the other is treating it as a mere act, the one attempting to show affection is most always left feeling empty because she is not getting from the act what she is giving.

I think about the story of Tamar and Amnon.   You will find it in the 13th chapter of 2nd Samuel.   Tamar was Amnon's half-sister.   She was one of King Solomon's most beautiful daughters.   Amnon actually fell in love with his sister.   Or perhaps it was just lust because of her beauty.   We don't really know.   Even so, feigning illness, Amnon tricked his father into allowing Tamar to tend to him.   Once he had her alone in his chambers, he raped her.   And this he did even after she nearly gave him her hand in marriage.

She told him to consult with their father and surely King Solomon would not keep her from him.   In other words, she was saying "don't just take advantage of me; do this the right way if you desire me in this way."   This may seem a stretch for the point I'm making but follow me.

After raping his sister, the bible states that he was filled with hatred towards her.   It goes further to state that the hatred he now had was even greater than the love that he had prior to forcing himself upon her.   He then had her dragged out of his chambers.   This was an act of extreme humiliation for the young woman.   Raped by her half-brother (they did not have the same mothers), and then rejected in such a cruel way.   The bible states that after these events, she "remained desolate" in her brother Absolom's house.   That word translated actually means devastated.   In other words, she remained devastated by this event and never married.

I questioned God about this event many times. The whole scene of Amnon's lust for Tamar that turned so quickly into absolute hatred baffled me. What was it that made him turn in such a cruel way? Could it be that he expected his sister to have the same sexual desire for him as he had for her? And being forced upon, she was in no position to reciprocate love or sexual gratification in any capacity—and certainly not toward her brother. The saddest part of the story is her desperate appeal to the brother she undoubtedly had sisterly affection for before this extremely traumatic experience. She says, *"Sending me away now is worse than what you've already done to me"* (NLT 2Sam 13:16).

He rejects her completely. So now she bears not only the shame of having been raped by her own brother, but the twisted perverted shame of being rejected sexually by this same man. And the end result is that she never marries, considering herself unclean I'm sure, and undoubtedly ashamed and acutely emotionally tormented.

This story shows an image of a woman sexually rejected. By all accounts, the real perversion lies in the fact that it is her brother lusting for her in the first place. But the image of sexual rejection is still present here. I can't say why Amnon was so cruel to Tamar. Tamar, herself, even asks "What's the reason for this?" As in "what's the reason for expelling me now that you have already done this thing?" Cruelty piled on top of more cruelty. In any event, Tamar would remain devastated having been betrayed by someone that she loved and trusted, made a spectacle of in front of her other siblings, and left to nurse a wound that's nearly impossible to heal. Sexual rejection can do all of this to any woman and even more.

In my sexual act with "old friend" I desired affection from him, but only got sex. I got only what he had come to expect from me—sex with no remorse, no recourse and no affection as its source. This was how we had related to one another nearly one year prior exactly to the moment that we were presently engaged in. Sex—no questions, no affirmations. Sex alone. And because my act of affection toward him was completely unanswered, I bore the brunt of extreme disappointment and rejection—completely unbeknownst to him. I was not only naked and ashamed literally, I was psychologically and emotionally tormented as well.

I was not only feeling the effects of years and years of trying to make a man "my man" by using my body, but also the keen awareness that I was being judged and critiqued on my sexual performance. Not only that, I was quite certain that this man was deciding whether to pursue a relationship with me based on how well I performed for him. And as discernment continued to kick in, I was not measuring up in this man's sexual estimation of me. This fact was gravely detrimental to me because I was so emotionally vested in this particular man.

I will never forget the humiliation I felt as I had myself

on my knees in front of this man (and not in a posture of prayer either). *Is this what I have to do to get you to love me? Is this all I'm worth to you? Is this all I'm worth—period?* These were some of the questions I wrestled with. Not because the act of oral sex is shameful to me—it's not. But the context of the act is what brought shame to me. I was not engaging in oral sex simply because I wanted to satisfy him in this way. I was performing oral sex out of a twisted desire to earn his approval and acceptance. As uncomfortable as I was in performing this sexual act, I still proceeded with it out of fear of further rejection. It was my choice.

I cannot and will not say that he forced me to perform oral sex. He did not. It was more of a mild unspoken demand on his part. There was a definite sense of, "either do this or nothing's going on between us." That could have been my supposed internal feeling, but he definitely imposed his penis on my mouth (feel free to gasp now—I understand this is heavy material). There was that awkward feeling of, "If I don't proceed in this act then certainly he's going to have nothing more to do with me." As if further rejection was even possible considering the extreme levels of rejection I had experienced with this man already. But alas, I would prove even myself wrong.

I need to insert this idea here: there is nothing wrong with oral sex, anal sex or any other kind of sex that a married man and woman has. I am so very tired of the church demonizing sexual practices and trying to construct and erect entire doctrines based on the erroneous idea that any type of sex other than missionary-style is sinful.   The truth is that the bible makes no commentary whatsoever on specific sexual practices. The bible does speak against fornication, homosexuality, and even bestiality.   But it does not name certain sexual positions or sexual styles as wrong or right.   There is no biblical proof anyone can find to support the idea that oral sex or anal sex are somehow ungodly.   I think it is fallacious and cruel to tell married couples how they should have sex.   God is not against whatever a married couple decides is right for them, with the exception, of course, of bringing other people into the marriage bed.   If you have a certain bent in favor or against particular sexual practices, that needs to be discussed with your spouse and God.   However, you cannot take your personal bent for or against certain sexual practices and form a Christian-based argument.   You won't find support in the bible to endorse your stance against particular sexual practices such as oral or anal sex.

It is high time that the church discuss sex among married people in a correct, biblically sound way.   And telling couples that oral sex and anal sex (if they choose to practice these) is wrong is not supported or ordained by God.   Again, you will not find in any bible proof to support oral sex as an act of ungodliness.   In fact, if God intended for sex organs only to be used for sex, then kissing would be outlawed and lips restricted only to speaking.   Hands would only be used to work with and hold—but not in a romantic way because that would indicate using hands for affection.

If you demonize one practice you must demonize them all. God is not in any of that. The only sex that is unlawful and can be considered unholy, ungodly and offensive to God is fornicative sex—sex between unmarried people, adulterous sex—sex between a married person and someone other than their spouse, and sex with people of the same gender—homosexuality. Having said this I must also insert another idea: marriage between homosexuals does not make sex between them lawful in the sight of God. Homosexuality is its own brand of sinfulness that has to be dealt with apart from their desire to marry.

WHEW!! I know I just covered a lot of ground and issues that you may not have been expecting, but I felt the need to address them here. Smile! And let's move on with my story.

After enduring the extreme humiliation of unreciprocated sexual gratification, the shame of feeling silently coerced to perform oral sex, and even the awareness that I was not sexually pleasing to this man, somehow, I still hoped and desired to be received by "old friend." All the while, knowing full well that I was not and would not be received by him. The ultimate end result of my final visit with "old friend" was a lonely flight home where I awaited a phone call or at least an acknowledgement of some sort to reassure me that my sore jaws and knees were not in vain.

To my chagrin, all was a loss. A loss of pride. A loss of confidence. A loss of self-esteem. An extreme loss of comfort in my nakedness.   I've got a pretty good feeling that this is how Tamar may have felt.   And perhaps even the woman at the well may have also felt this way in each one of her five marriages—LOST.

I had taken my panties off once more for this man and he could care less about me.   The excruciating, tormenting, exigent travail I felt was a pain I can't fully describe in words.   I opened my heart to this man.   I shared my dreams with him. I lowered myself to degrees of shamefulness I had never known before—all to no avail.   I cried and cried for days, weeks and months without end.

The only truth I could acknowledge was that "old friend" did not deserve my panties.   A dear friend told me, "he was not worthy of you."   And certainly I did not feel that way.   I actually felt unworthy of **him**.   He did not deserve my complete utter nakedness that I willingly gave to him.   He hadn't even earned it.   Yet I was the one feeling unworthy and small because I willingly gave my panties to him once again.   Why was it so easy for me to fall back into such a destructive pattern with this man?   Why could I so quickly forget that I'm a saved woman who really does love Jesus?

I know, "waa waa waa" you're probably thinking by now. Or even, "girl you asked for that one."   Whether I welcomed the wounds with carelessness or fell victim to some man's malice, the pain hurts all the same.   And my heart hurt very, very deeply. One reason I was able to slip back into such a seemingly obvious destructive pattern with "old friend" is because of the phenomenon known as a "soul-tie." Now before you get all churchy on me let me explain this as God has revealed it to me. The term soul-tie is nowhere in the bible. You will not find that term. There is instead the term "knit" or woven. This type of bond occurred between two individuals I have already mentioned and they were neither related nor married. In fact, they were the same sex. And NO they were not homosexual; and I am in no way making a case for homosexuality. I'm talking about David and Jonathon; they were merely really good friends.

Most Christian people will contend that a soul-tie is established through the act of having sex. I come to mess with that ideology for a minute because God has shown me something different. It was easy for me to run back to "old friend" because my soul was indeed tied to his. But it had very little to do with the sex that took place between us. My soul had been connected to this man for years before we ever touched. How is that? All the church folk ask. Well, remember I shared earlier that he was my first love.

Therefore, many years before our sexual encounter, we had shared soulish issues with one another. That little process of getting-to-know someone that includes sharing your innermost feelings and desires—all that good stuff falls into the category of soulish issues. I opened my mind, my emotions and my heart to this man long before I had sex with him. That is how a genuine soul-tie was established. That is how any genuine soul-tie is generated—the sharing of soulish issues. Or issues relating to your soul—the innermost part of whom you are.

You need to know that your soul is made up of your inner self—your thoughts-**mind**, your intentions and decisions-**will**, and your feelings-**emotions**. These elements together comprise your soul, or the very deepest part of who you are. When you engage these elements with someone, you engage your soul with that person. This is done by being transparent and naked with them emotionally. When you reveal your true self to someone in an intimate way you are, in effect, opening your soul. When that person reciprocates this act, an exchange of soulish issues occurs.

All of this is taking place emotionally and mentally without even physically touching in any way. These are the strongest bonds to create—those in which the soul is completely engaged. In fact, the only types of genuine soul-ties ever mentioned in the bible happen to have occurred between individuals of the same sex. Now you must know that these relationships were not homosexual by any means. They are simply biblical representations of what a genuine "soul-tie" looks like. A father and his son. A widow and her mother-in-law. A man exiled by the king and the king's son.

To be sure, sex alone is not enough to generate a deep genuine soul-tie. I will not deny that sex can certainly reinforce an existing soul-tie. But simply having sex joins you to a person in a different way. Something beyond the physical act of sex definitely happens when you participate in it. But that is more of an exchange of natures and knowledge than a joining of souls. The person you're having sex with receives knowledge about you as well as a piece of your nature or personality traits, and vice versa. I'm about to get real deep and controversial, so hold on.

The bible never uses the term "sex." Instead, it uses the word "know" when referring to sexual intercourse. As I understand it, and as I believe God has revealed to me, having sex is an exchange of knowledge about the participating parties. It is definitely a way of becoming one, or uniting with another person as well. However, I do not want to go into an in-depth study about the act of "becoming one" in marriage. I will say this: sex was given to married couples by God. By all accounts it is a marriage rite—or privilege.

God designed sex to happen after a couple married in order to signify their oneness and to seal their wedding vows. When sex happens outside of marriage vows, fornication occurs. Having sex apart from marriage vows is still a signal of oneness though. Essentially, you are illegally partaking of the rites of marriage without entering into the contract of marriage. But again, this act of oneness does not constitute a soul-tie.

On the other hand, it is possible to have a soul-tie to sex itself. I told you I was gonna mess with what you think you know. When sex is pleasurable and good, you intuitively engage your emotions in the act. That is to say, you *like* the experience. So much so, that you will begin to *desire* the *experience* of sex simply for the good-feeling it gives you. Your feelings are inherently engaged when the sex is good. In addition, because many women have difficulties reaching an orgasm, having sex with a man who helps her "get there" can almost feel like being cared about. A woman can misread a sexual experience as an emotional experience. Continuing to indulge in repeat good-sex strengthens the emotional bond she has developed with SEX—not even the person she may be having it with in many cases—just the mere act alone.

Hence, a soul-tie to sex has developed because she has engaged her emotions on a deep level, and has engaged her *will* because she *chooses* to keep having sexual experiences hoping to generate that great feeling again and again. This includes sex a person has with herself or masturbation. Yes—you can have a soul-tie to masturbation as well.

Now, what makes masturbation so detrimental to our souls is the perversion of sex that it represents. God did not design our bodies to sexually gratify itself. However, our bodies can't help what they like and what feels good to them. Once a person begins to self-satisfy, she is going to develop an emotional attachment to it—an addiction. Here is the awkward moment: the bible doesn't speak against masturbation. You are not going to find any commentary about sex with the self in the bible.

And many people will use this fact as a means to

continue to engage in masturbation—I did. Something else that makes masturbation a perversion is the fact that a person must have a mental image in order to facilitate it—a fantasy. You have to force sexual imagery into your mind in order to experience an orgasm from masturbation. In so doing, you are literally sexually assaulting the Holy Spirit that lives inside of you by forcing Him to partake of the sexual images that you replay in your mind. Indulging in pornography is the same thing: forcing sexual imagery onto the Holy Spirit within you.

For unmarried folk, fantasizing about sex is meditating on sin because if you're not married sex for you is sinful. For MARRIED folk, having sex with yourself is actually cheating on your husband. Sure it is. You are essentially telling your spouse he is incapable of sexually satisfying you and that you can do a better job of it.

And by all accounts, once a person has developed a soul-tie to masturbation, no other form of sexual gratification will suffice. Having learned to do certain sexual things to herself that a penis was not designed to do, a woman will ultimately no longer desire the sexual gratification that her husband is supposed to provide. That person will continually reach further into depths of perversion attempting to be sexually satisfied, further reinforcing the soul-tie to masturbation.

Let me to go ahead and make it all the way real: masturbation is selfish. It is putting your own desires and preferences above God's design for sex. We can try to justify it, but the real truth is that we like it (for those of us who have practiced masturbation). We enjoy the immediate sexual high it gives. It has become a comfort to us and a companion to us. I'm not crazy; I know that there are women who will use (and DO use) masturbation as a means to not engage in fornication (NO, it is not OK to do that). This is extremely dangerous because of the emotional attachment that develops. The truth is this: once you start on the course of using masturbation as a means of sexual gratification it will be hard to stop, just as it is with any addiction. In fact, that's really what addictions are: wrongful soul-ties to certain things or practices.

However, soul-ties with people are a little different. Unless your mind, will and emotions are engaged and vested with a person, to the degree you feel unexplainably "bound" to him, you do not have a soul-tie with him. Yes, you can have sex with a person and never establish a binding of your soul with him. Think about any time you may have had sex with someone and immediately forgot that person's very existence soon after the break-up. Or even, the fact that men can so easily be completely emotionally UN-engaged with the act of sex. This is proof that unless your emotions are engaged in the act of sex on a deep level, a genuine soul-tie will not be established.

Genuinely tying your soul to someone not only engages your innermost self, but also your affections. Recall the discussion I had about your affections in chapter 1. The issue with your affections is that they are guided by your heart. Your heart is the part of you that believes. *"For with the heart one believes unto righteousness. . ."* (Rom10:10). Your mind is what does your "knowing." Your emotions are what do your "feeling." Your will is what does your "deciding." And your heart is how you do your "believing." Your heart is directly tied to your affections. Many times in the bible when God is referring to "affections" He uses the word "heart." In Matthew 15:8, it says *"This people draweth nigh unto me with their mouth . . . but their heart is far from me."* The translation of this word used for "heart" is actually "affections." This is why you can't take your panties off for just anyone.

When you get utterly naked emotionally you expose your soul and your heart; and the innermost part of who you are is at risk of being incredibly wounded. This is why God warns *"Keep (Guard) your heart with all diligence for out of it are the issues of life"* (Proverbs 4:23-emphasis mine). Your heart actually guides your life. And you function in life by way of your soul—your knowledge, choices and feelings. Your heart leads your soul in its many functions. What the heart believes the soul enacts. And from your heart proceed your affections—or passion. You see, your heart is where your passions are stored also.

Your heart decides what you are passionate about or affectionate toward. Not your knowledge. Not your feelings. Not your decisions. All of these can provide worthy information that may sway you one way or the other, but ultimately your heart is what *passionately* or *affectionately*

BELIEVES the information being given it.

Why all the talk about passions, affections and the heart? Because all of these will determine how you relate to a man and ultimately to God.   Not only that, but also how you identify and relate to yourself.   When any area of your soul is wounded life is going to be a little more than difficult to endure.   And when your heart is wounded in addition to that, life is almost unlivable. God says, *"The spirit of man will sustain his infirmity, but a wounded spirit who can bear?"* (Proverbs 18:14 emphasis mine) What you need to know about God is that whenever He asks the question "Who can . . ." do this or that, the answer is actually NOONE except Him.   This verse is saying that a person with a strong spirit will be able to endure being wounded or offended or hurt, but when the spirit is what is wounded then there's an even bigger issue to deal with.

Ok, so what does my spirit have to do with my heart? Well, the bible says, *"a merry heart makes a cheerful countenance, but by sorrow of the heart the spirit is broken"* (Proverbs 15:13 emphasis mine).   So then, a person's heart is somehow connected to their spirit as well.   And having sorrow in one's heart is directly proportionate to a person's ability to sustain woundedness.   When your heart is sorrowful or broken your spirit is broken.   When your spirit is broken you cannot sustain woundedness of any degree.

And when you are incapable of enduring woundedness your life is difficult to live.   This is why having a broken heart is one of the most dangerous and important types of wounds to Jesus. When your heart is wounded your belief system is haywire and untrustworthy; and your life follows suit by design. Look at it this way: broken heart=broken spirit=inability to sustain hurts=crippled ability to function in life.

Giving my panties to "old friend" both literally and emotionally left me wounded in the worst possible way a woman can be wounded—brokenhearted. You see, I expected "old friend" to be the type of friend that I outlined in the beginning of this chapter—one who had qualified for my nakedness. But the real truth is that he had neither qualified for such a position nor was even interested in having such a place in my life. God had indeed given me clues about delving into depths of nakedness with "old friend," but I was too lonely to heed those.

Instead, I was willing to ascribe qualification to "old friend" in order to suit my immediate needs. Loneliness. Companionless. Affectionless. This proved to be extremely detrimental to my spiritual, psychological and emotional health. My entire life as a whole was jeopardized—literally. Ultimately, while I was looking to "old friend" to be my qualified comfort-in-nakedness companion, he actually was the very antithesis. I ended up needing a genuinely qualified friend to help pull me out of the pit of utter despair I had crept into due to my crushed hopes and wounded soul and broken heart. This is where my dear sister-friend came to my rescue.

Having forged a genuine strong soul-tie with this man

many years prior, and then reinforcing that bond with sex, the healing process was very slow and painful. In fact, I'm still in that process even right now. I shared soulish issues with "old friend". I shared life issues with him. I shared affections with him and engaged my heart and soul and body with him. That's three distinct parts of who I am. The bible states in Ecclesiates 4:12 that *"a threefold cord is not **quickly** broken"* (emphasis mine). Those three cords can be your mind, will and emotions. Or they could be your heart, soul and body. Either way, it's a threefold cord; and the severing of that bond will not happen "quickly."

I was thoroughly bound to "old friend." I expected to marry this man. And because I was so knotted to him in every conceivable way a person can be tied to another, I was left devastated by his complete and utter rejection of me. Sexually rejected. Emotionally rejected. Absolutely rejected in every possible way a person can be. Life got nearly unlivable for me after this immense bout of rejection. And it is from this position that God is even right now picking me back up. It still hurts—it hurts like hell on hot wheels taking a bath in vinegar. But I am persuaded that He who has begun this work of restoration in me is faithful to see me through to the end. And if you happen to number yourself in this party, there is hope for you too.

The story of me and "old friend" has ended, but the story of me and Jesus is still in progress—and I don't expect it to end any time soon.

Chapter 4

So Who Needs Panties Anyway???

*G*o ahead and breathe. Soul-ties-and-passions-and-panties—O H MY! I know that was deep water to tread in, but I had to go there. Having shared all of that nakedness with you, you now may be inclined to wonder, "so who needs panties anyway?—especially if 'it's OK to be naked'?" Well, just as nakedness serves a crucial purpose, panties likewise serve a critical purpose. It was only after arriving at the truth about their situation that God was moved to cover Adam and Eve.

It was only after the true acknowledgement of herself and her authentic circumstance that the Canaanite woman was able to receive Jesus' covering—His grace. The purpose of panties you ask? To cover your shame. To remove it from you and give you comfort. To restore in you the confidence you need in order to be in God's presence. And who needs all of that? You do. I do. We need panties. We just need to know where to get them and Who to get them from.

Let me tell you about Ruth. Yeah, I know you think you know this story already, but let me give you a new perspective on it. Ruth was a Moabitess. She was from the city of Moab whose culture was much like that of the Canaanite woman we discussed earlier except, Moab was to the extreme in idolatry. You will have to read the whole story of Ruth in the book of the bible named for her. Here's a brief synopsis: Ruth moved to Bethlehem with her mother-in-law, Naomi, after the deaths of both of their husbands.

Ruth then, unknowingly, began to work in the fields of Boaz—a wealthy Jewish man who happened to be a relative of her dead husband and father-in-law. Boaz asks his workers about her identity, and she is brought before him in their presence. He refers to Ruth as a "damsel," which indicates that she must be much younger than he and most likely around the same age as his workers. This is important to notice. Ruth definitely wanted to be married again. A young widow was regarded very harshly in Hebrew culture. But Ruth was also an outcast to the Jewish people, being of an idolatrous background and a person of very low status having no male heir.

Aware of Ruth's past, Boaz speaks very highly of her in the presence of the young men and women who work for him. Ruth noticed this act of kindness. So much so, that she in turn lies to her mother-in-law about the arrangement she had made with Boaz. He had told Ruth to stay close to his female workers throughout the harvesting season. But Ruth tells Naomi that Boaz told her to stay close to his *young men.* I struggled with this passage. *Why would she lie?* I had to question God about it several times. He gave me the answer. Ruth took Boaz's act of complimenting her in front of the young men as him cleaning up her image so that they would not reject her and hopefully favor her enough to consider marriage material.

His compliment may have also helped to take away the alienation she might have experienced from the other women as well. Boaz took away the shamefulness Ruth may have felt from being a widowed stranger by speaking very highly of her in the presence of his own people. This was the first time that he covered Ruth. This sounds a lot like Jesus and the Canaanite woman to me. The covering of known nakedness or shamefulness brings *comfort.* Are you following? Hold on, because it gets deeper.

By lying to Naomi about the arrangement with Boaz and the reapers, Ruth may have merely been attempting to secure her own future. In accordance, I believe that Naomi saw through that idea and offered Ruth some motherly wisdom. She told

Ruth it would be better for her to work near the young women, as Boaz had originally explained to Ruth unbeknownst to Naomi. She explained to Ruth that she would be safer this way. Naomi might have been bitter and at ought with God but she certainly was not crazy and oblivious. Like Boaz, she was actually protecting Ruth's image as well. She knew the dangers that awaited a young foreign woman in the presence of young men. Ruth was apt to agree and did as Naomi had instructed her to do.

Even so, Naomi recognized Ruth's fear of rejection and set in order the plan for Ruth to marry Boaz. She gave Ruth some very specific instructions to follow, being moved to ensure Ruth's *future*. This is where the story takes an interesting turn. Naomi tells Ruth to bathe herself and anoint herself *and* present herself to Boaz SECRETLY after he has had his evening wine. At first it sounds almost innocent. Ruth has been in the fields all day and naturally she probably stinks and needs to change her panties anyway. Right? Well, all of that would be great if I didn't happen to know that a woman bathing and anointing herself and then going to see A MAN, in this culture, is actually more than likely a solicitation for sex.

And if not sex at that moment, at the very least, Ruth was presenting herself as an available, beautiful young woman to an older unmarried WEALTHY man. And don't forget this: Ruth is doing all of this IN A PRIVATE AREA, while NOONE ELSE IS THERE. So you gotta ask yourself, what was she doing? Of course, historically and culturally we can say that Boaz was the closest of kin and he had to perform the traditional

Jewish death-of-husband-redemption rites—yaada yaada yaada. Can it also be said that Ruth was certainly trying to make a grand appeal for herself to that end?   Now, consider this: Since it was Naomi who told her to do these things in this manner, how do you think Ruth felt about that?   Feel free to SELAH right about now.

Here's what also needs to be taken into account: Ruth has already expressed her interest in the *young men*—albeit a gentle expression of interest; Boaz entreats her as a daughter so I must believe she sees him more as a father-figure than anything else; and she comes from a culture where women perform sexual acts with men in practice of idol-worship and are treated with the utmost disrespect because of this.

Add all of this to the fact that she thought she had escaped her former culture by choosing to stay with Naomi who is now seemingly telling her to revert to her former cultural standards of sex and relating to men.   You don't think that Ruth may have felt just a tad bit ashamed to present herself in *this* manner to *this* man that she has garnered so much respect for?   When I consider all of these issues surrounding Ruth, the story takes on a whole new meaning.   You see, even though Naomi's plan started off a little awkward, it still ended beautifully—we all know that.

But here is where the real beauty is showcased; Boaz did not cause Ruth any further shame.   When Ruth, being obedient to Naomi, presented herself to Boaz in the middle of the night, he did not take her gestures for granted and take opportunity to treat her as a woman desperate for a husband. He didn't deal with her according to her past either. If Boaz were a dirty-old-man interested in a quick cheap thrill, he could have easily reminded Ruth of her Moabitish background and demanded she do whatever he wanted her to do in order to satisfy him and thereby persuade him to perform the redemption rites. And if I could go ahead and be honest yet again, I have to say that I think Naomi could have had all of this in mind when she told Ruth what to do with Boaz.

After all, Naomi tells Ruth "he will tell you what you *shall* (must) do" (Ruth 3:4 emphasis mine). As if to say, "whatever he wants you to do—GIRL—you better be like NIKE and just do it!" That is, once Boaz was good and full and a little "merry with wine," his temperament would be such that, not only could he be easily swayed to action at the sight of a beautiful young woman, but also moved to command her as he wished knowing the depth of her desperation. But he didn't make Ruth do anything to earn a position of worthiness with him. REMEMBER THAT.

Boaz didn't give Ruth a list of requirements to adhere to. He didn't make her feel more uncomfortable than she undoubtedly already felt at that crucial moment. He covered her. Literally. Emotionally. And spiritually. He recognized the nakedness and courage it took for her to come to him and he did not mishandle it—he shielded and protected it. His action was actually more inline of that which a father would take on his daughter's behalf. That's true friendship. That's true love beyond mere redemption. That's genuine regard for another's character.

What I see in this story is God's tenderness in dealing with our human deficits and shame. Ruth may have been a new convert to Jewish culture and standards, but don't think for one moment that she completely forgot where she came from. This fact is evident in the story when she first meets Boaz and describes herself as a "stranger." This is no different than the shame many of us feel as we recall our former or even current lifestyles. We count ourselves unworthy of God's grace and love. We forget that LOVE is not something that God DOES. It is Who He IS. God is love.

We say that casually and toss it around in such cliché fashion, but we need to genuinely understand what it means for God to BE love. Because He is love, He can do nothing except show love to His children. He is forced to respond to the cries of the hurting. He is moved to action by the broken hearted. God understands that we must feel comfort if we are going to receive covering. These are the very reasons Jesus came to the earth—to show the love of God to the hurting and brokenhearted; to take away the guilt that sin causes people to feel; and to cover the shame that sin consciousness causes.

What does God's love and grace have to do with my sexual issues? ABSOLUTELY EVERYTHING!! Here is my truth: nearly every single sexual experience I have ever had in my life was an attempt by me to gain some form of comfort. I either wanted to be consoled after the death of my father and grandfather, or I wanted to be held because life was spinning out of control, or I wanted to "feel like a natural woman" because I just got tired of waiting to be found. In some way I wanted to be comforted by someone. And when someone was not available I settled for some *THING*. That "thing" with which I tried to comfort myself could have been a vibrator. It could have been a pornographic website. It could have been a sexual fantasy. It could have been "that one dude" I saw at the mall one day. It could have been that "old friend" I ran into on Facebook. It could have been that last glass of wine. It could have been that last piece of cake or plate of food. It could have been . . . anything. For me, it was sex (most of the time) or something very close to it—masturbation, pornography. What my soul really wanted and desperately needed was and is comfort.

In all of my trying to alleviate my own sorrow, I was actually creating another form of grief—the grief of known sinfulness. When you are alive to Christ you cannot knowingly walk into sin without feeling some kind of way about it. There is a struggle. There is an awareness of wrongness. You know exactly what you're doing.

You may be powerless to prevent yourself from engaging. You may not be privy to the "why," but somewhere on the inside of you a fight is definitely going on if you are truly saved. I will go as far as to even say, you may not necessarily know how you came to such a pass or know how to stop.   But believe me; when you are a saved person who enters into sinfulness, you are quite aware that something's just not right. The truth is that you enter into sinfulness attempting to comfort yourself.   And because you are aware of the wrongness of your actions, you in turn need to comfort yourself a little more from the shame that that knowledge brings.

Here is a fact of life: when we attempt to comfort ourselves we will always remain with a deficit.   Comfort can't come from the outside in only.   Not lasting comfort.   Not real comfort.   A hug may satiate you for the moment that you are being embraced, but when the other person's arms are no longer there, you will still feel a void.

This is because genuine comfort must go deeper than what we see and experience.   It must get to your heart because that is what is really hurting anyway.   A hug cannot make it to your heart unless you believe that the person who gave it really loves you even after they are no longer holding you.   But what happens when they walk away?

Here is some more truth to digest: there is no penis large enough long enough thick enough to penetrate me deep enough to fill the gaping hole in my heart created by decades of unhealed wounds (gasp if you need to).   And I have tried and tried to find one all to no avail.   In the end I'm even less comforted than I was before I engaged in some sinful sexual act.   WHY? Because a penis was not designed to comfort me—not in the way

I really need to be comforted, and certainly not when that particular penis does not belong to my husband. A man's sexual member was not designed to heal my heart. Masturbation cannot heal my heart. Pornography cannot heal my heart. Sexual fantasies cannot heal my heart. That's God's job and His alone. Applying this truth to my heart is harder than I thought.

One main reason for this is because I have grown accustomed to instant gratification. That's what sex does for me. That's what pornography does for me; it instantly gratifies me for a few seconds. We live in a generation where everything we desire can be at our fingertips in an instant. Just look at all the fast-food chains around the world. People enjoy convenience and expedited gratification. Therefore, people expect instant healing and deliverance as well. I am absolutely convinced that God is more than able to perform instant miracles and overnight blessings—I have personally been a recipient of many.

However, God does not operate in automaticity all of the time. And to expect Him to do so is to treat Him like a genie or magician. By doing this we limit God to performing "on demand," and refuse to learn how to trust Him in patience. And believe me, you are going to need to trust God patiently in most things in your life. I have heard someone say, "God is never late, but He's never early either." It's easy to seek temporal comfort in sex, food or whatever pleasure gives you comfort for the moment. But learning to receive comfort from

God, whom you cannot see, is not as easy as some people make it sound. It is a matter of relearning what genuine affection is—or learning what it is in the first place. It is a matter of undoing years and decades of *mis*comforting ourselves.

You see, once we have grown accustomed to comforting ourselves for so long in certain ways, we know no other way of being comforted. Try telling someone addicted to drugs to just "STOP DOING DRUGS" and see how far that goes. Addictions are a means of comfort for many people. Sex is no different. Pornography is no different. Masturbation is no different. Food is no different. Shopping is no different. These are all external attempts to ease an internal ailment—ailments that we have carried on the inside of us for years and years.

Wounds that we may not even know are still open and oozing with the discomfort of infection. These wounds on our soul lead us into comfort-seeking. This pain on the inside of us could be from being told our lips are too big, our hair is too nappy, our hair is too straight, we have too many freckles, our lips are too thin. It could also be from never being told that we're beautiful, capable, creative, and intelligent.

All of these seemingly minor soul-lacerations create open sores that need attention. And after years and years of ignoring that sore, that wound, we live our lives as if it didn't matter—as if the hurt didn't matter. "Oh that little thing?—aaw it's nothing. . ." But it *was* something dear one. It *is* something.   And something serious enough to still affect how you perceive yourself today.   How you relate to your world today.   How you relate to men today.   How you relate to other women today.   And most importantly, how you relate to God today.   Here's another truth: you wear a different set of panties for each relationship you're engaged in.   And whatever panties you're wearing right now is evidence of the attempts to comfort yourself from the pain that you thought meant nothing.

The "sexy panties"—the garments you wear attempting to illicit compliments when all the while on the inside you don't really know that you're beautiful with or without that tight-fitting   or   low-cut   attire.   The   "comfortable panties"—you're fine and nothing's wrong in your life that you cannot control when all the while your life is actually spinning as far away from "control" as possible.   All of these panties are masks and costumes that we put on and then attempt to relate to God and our world.   The problem with this is that we're actually hiding.

But here is some real comfort: God is not unaware of all of THAT.   God is not up in heaven blind deaf and dumb to our human condition or the course of our lives.   God knows exactly how you ended up the way that you are today.   And by supernatural wisdom and genuine tenderness He absolutely knows what it takes to get you out of whatever you're in today. He is absolutely aware of the things people do to comfort themselves either because they know no other means, or because they haven't grown into trusting Him in that capacity.

Yes—God can handle you not yet trusting Him. The bible is replete with instances of God proving to man His trustworthiness. From David and his victories in battle to the prophet Elijah and his victories over Ahab, God desires to be trusted and doesn't mind proving to us that He can be. If you start in the book of Genesis with our favorite couple of discussion, Adam and Eve, you will find evidence of God willing to prove His faithfulness to His children.

As a matter of fact, I'm pretty sure you can probably search your own history and discover the times that God has shown up in your life when no one else was there. Remind yourself of God's faithfulness TO YOU. If you're reading this right now, you're alive and that fact alone means God is not through showing Himself able to be trusted in your life.

God completely absolutely intends to comfort wounded hearts, broken spirits, and painful pasts. *How do we know this?* He has said so Himself. He has shown us through Jesus. The very first proclamation that Jesus made to announce His ministry to a congregation of people was:

> *The Spirit of The Lord is upon me because He has anointed me to preach the gospel to the poor; He hath sent me to heal the brokenhearted, to preach* **deliverance to the captives,** *recovery of sight to the blind, to* **set at liberty them that are bruised** (Luke 4:18 emphasis mine).

This is the image of God comforting His people. This is what God wants us to know about what He has done through the life of Jesus and what he continues to do through the blood of Jesus. This is what Jesus was dying to tell us about God our Father.

Let's take a closer look at this passage. The last word of this passage, "bruised," is in the bible only one time—this time. Its literal translation is "crushed in pieces by calamity." I think we all need a SELAH right here. Ever felt crushed? Ever felt like you were in pieces? Have you ever felt like calamities were outnumbering you and pressing you down? GOOD!

That is what Jesus came to liberate you from—the bruises of life. Those wounds that were given to us in childhood. Those bruises that the wrong man left on our hearts. Those open sores that have remained no matter the amount of fasting, praying, anointing with oil or running around churches—these are the reasons Jesus decided to come to the earth and willingly die for us. To heal our broken hearts. To deliver us from captivity. And to set us at liberty. Those last two almost sound like the same thing. Yet they must not be the same if Jesus has them distinctly separated in different phraseology. Apparently, you can be free and UN-liberated.

That is to say, you can be saved and still in captivity. Perhaps the common word for captivity needs to be applied here: BONDAGE. Oooh . . . I know that's a nasty word in church, but too many Christians are yet wrapped up in things that they still need to be liberated from. And the unraveling process is not an easy one.   It's not as simple as someone merely praying a prayer over you or with you, and you returning home and everything in life is fine and dandy.   On the contrary, when a person is bound up in some soulish manner, it can take years before real freedom will begin to manifest.   This is because oftentimes, many people don't know that they aren't fully liberated and they don't know what the liberation process looks like.   They go to church every Sunday.   They attend bible study regularly.

And for some reason they're trying to figure out why they snap at their kids.   Or why they snap at random people. It doesn't have to be "snapping" on someone.   Perhaps they struggle with doubting God—that He really loves them.   Or maybe they struggle with being trusting of other people. Perhaps they struggle with not feeling, believing and KNOWING they are beautiful, strong and wise.   Whatever the struggle is, it is actually a symptom of bondage existing in an area of someone's life.

So what does being in bondage have to do with my panties?   If you find yourself leaving your panties with random men at various times . . . YOU ARE IN BONDAGE HUN!   But not solely of your own creating.   The type of bondage that leads us into behaviors that are contradictory to our best selves is bondage that we were, at some point in our lives, powerless to prevent.   You can't prevent being picked on by kids at school when you're a child.   You can't prevent parents that walk away from the responsibility of taking care of their children.   You can't prevent your heart from being broken by some man who has yet to figure out what loving you really looks like. You can't prevent friends from lying to you and on you. You can't prevent many of the hurts that were heaped upon you as you traversed through life up to this point. These are the wounds that just came our way. And we were powerless to prevent them—and God knows this. This is why we seek comfort. And this is why God is so compassionate toward us.

GOD desires that we know He loves us in our broken piecemeal state, so instead of beating us into submission of His word, He chooses to cover us in our often, OFTEN transgressing. He has seen how we arrived at our present condition. He has watched while we were antagonized by the enemy. He has witnessed how we were trodden under the heavy foot of disappointment. And just as Boaz would not allow Ruth to be made to feel ashamed for who she was beside the widow of a Jewish man, God will not allow us to be made ashamed of who we were and who we are right at this very moment.

In my heart, I believe God remembers the frailty and innocent ignorance of Adam and Eve when He sees us seeking comfort in things apart from Him. He sees us wanting to relieve the pain that is a constant in our lives. I believe God recalls the words of Jesus as He died on the cross, *"Father, forgive them for they know not what they do"* (Luke 23:34).

We must go back to Adam and Eve. When they brought sinfulness into the earth through their disobedience,

God was moved to cover them so that they would not feel the shame that their own act caused them to feel. Weird huh? They were absolutely guilty but God didn't want them to feel ashamed. That's because God is about *covering* shame not *causing* shame. However, God absolutely must *confront* shame. Just as He had to confront Adam and Eve, God in like manner must confront the shame in our lives. While they believed that the only problem was their lack of clothing, God knew the real issue was that they were ashamed of themselves for what they had done. God will expose shame to us in order to show us that we need Him and to bring us to a place of decision.

Shame causes fear and makes you want to hide—just as Adam and Eve did. But if we can recognize that there is no reason to hide from God we will enter into a completely different way of relating to Him. God, Himself, desires to be our ultimate hiding place. The bible says in Deuteronomy 33:27, *"The eternal God is your refuge, and His everlasting arms are under you"* (NKV emphasis mine). This term "refuge" is in reference to a designated place for people to flee to if they had committed a crime. God had instructed the Israelites to establish "cities of refuge," in order to give the guilty a place of restoration and a place to hide from those who sought vengeance (Numbers 35: 6).

It is in that place that comfort manifests. Also, in this place of refuge, God is holding you up in His arms. God has designated Himself as our personal "city of refuge," and by His own hands He upholds and comforts us. The second part of Deuteronomy 33:27 states, *"He drives out the enemy before thee; He cries out Destroy them."* "Them" meaning your enemies, and SHAME is one of our primary enemies. God has promised to drive out and destroy SHAME.

We must know that God will not exploit our nakedness. He deals gently with us when we are uncovered and exposed. He honors our willingness to move toward Him even while we feel ashamed.

Does everybody know the story of the woman with "the issue"? This story is found in the books of Matthew, Mark and Luke; but I think Mark's account is the best—find it in chapter 5. In any case, this nameless woman is ill with a nonstop flow of blood that has persisted over the course of twelve years. 12 years. Ladies imagine having a menstrual cycle that does not end from year to year. Your body being drained of life day after day. Your energy sapped. You can't even make love to your husband (if she was married). Because Hebrew cultural standards deemed her unclean, she was cast out of the community as well.

She was forced to live outside of the city limits and unable to enjoy physical human contact, let alone mere social contact. I wonder if any of her friends came to visit. I wonder if her husband still made her feel loved. This woman knew something about shame. This woman knew something about unclean panties. One day she crept into the city limits through throngs of people knowing that if she was discovered certain punishment would meet her.   She was completely aware of the Jewish laws surrounding her situation.   She knew that to touch another human automatically made that person unclean as well.   Shame.   Discomfort.   Humiliation.   Fear.   Yeah—she had some issues alright.   Being sick was only one of them.

With all of her shame, discomfort and humiliation she crept on toward Jesus.   The Man she had heard about.   I have heard so many reasons as to why she only touched the hem of His garment, but let me give you a few more.   Perhaps she thought that to touch His person would possibly make Him unclean too.   After all, she had only heard about Him—she didn't *know* Him.

Maybe she thought that He would not want to touch her.   It could be that she really didn't want to be noticed outside of her mandated perimeter.   She was ashamed.   Ashamed to have lived so long with an incurable disease that cost her her life's savings.   Ashamed that she couldn't sit and talk with other women.   Ashamed, believing that she had been cursed in this horrible way.   Ashamed.   But God saw and heard her.   For all of those 12 years He had watched her.   And at this moment He was still gazing in her direction.   He would not allow shame to prevent this woman from enjoying the benefits of salvation.   Don't forget that.

When Jesus inquired, "who touched me?" He wasn't

asking because He didn't know the answer. He was asking in order to confront the shame she felt on the inside of her.   Jesus wanted to give her the opportunity to either stand-up and shun the shame or flee.   She could have cowered and ran away with her healed self because she was instantly healed the moment she touched the garment of Jesus.   But she didn't run away.   She didn't *hide* herself; she was forced into ripping her own panties off and exposing the truth and the shame.

Understand this: everyone in the community knows who this woman is and what her issues were.   And all of them are watching this scene right now.   You don't think that those onlookers wanted to put her back in her "proper place"—outside the city walls?   Perhaps they even felt a level of shame themselves for this woman who was so desperate as to actually come crawling into the city limits with all of her mess.   You don't think that all of those people had heard Jesus inquire about who touched him?   Do you think that no one was aware that she was following Jesus?

She *was* FOLLOWING Jesus.   Crippled and doubled over in pain—she was following Jesus.   Stinking and fuming with blood soaked under garments—she was following Jesus. Scared and ashamed—she was following Jesus.   And He knew it too.   In this critical moment this woman is literally on the verge of death.   She could have been stoned to death for touching the person of someone with such stature as Jesus.

His response to her is all at once a confrontation and a

consolation. Jesus had to deal with the shame "issue" first. This nameless and now shameless woman must make a critical decision. Will she publicly uncover herself? Or will she silently walk back home? Remember this: she didn't have to reveal her identity. When the townspeople recognized who she really was, they could have arrested her on the spot. But they wanted to see the reaction of the "offended" Person—Jesus. Had He been truly offended by her touch, the people in this community would have had reason to deal harshly with other people like her and their issues.

Jesus had to be the example of covering compassion. He did not mishandle this woman's nakedness. He covered it. Once the shame was confronted, Jesus quickly moved in to console this woman. He said to her, *"daughter, thy faith hath made thee whole"* (Mk 5:34). In this moment Jesus doesn't just call her some generic daughter. He calls her a daughter of Abraham. That is, a daughter of promise. A chosen daughter. A daughter with the covenant guarantee of protection and safety and healing—salvation. Jesus reminded her of who she really is.

Why? Because wounded people need comfort. Wounded people often forget who they really are. Wounded people still have rights as sons and daughters of God—if they are God's people, that is, saved. God's wounded children are still God's children. I also believe that Jesus wanted her to know that there was nothing to be ashamed of. She was in need of health. She was in need of life. She was a daughter with a promise, and she came to the right place to get what she needed. The shame came from the way others made her feel about what was "wrong" with her. Did this woman have issues? Absolutely. Did this woman have some ongoing illness? Indeed she did. Are any of these reasons to be ashamed? Absolutely not. Jesus came to heal the bruised. Jesus came for those with "issues."

But just as there were people who wanted to keep this woman away from Jesus, there are people today who would rather keep hurting, broken people at a distance never receiving what they need from the Father who wants to give it. Luke 12:32 states, "fear not little flock, for it is your *Father's* good pleasure to give you the kingdom." This is Jesus speaking. He wants us to know that it gives God great pleasure to bestow upon us the kingdom of God.

This word "kingdom" can be misinterpreted to mean riches or wealth. That's not what Jesus is saying here (although He is NOT against wealth). Jesus is speaking about the rights and privileges afforded to us as heirs of the kingdom of God. Those rights include: protection, safety, health, healing, and preservation, just to name a few. Basically, all the entitlements of salvation are in tandem with the kingdom of God. And these God willingly desires to give us and allow us to operate in.

Just as Jesus had to remind the woman with the issue of her proper identity in relation to what was rightfully hers, Jesus reminds us here of our identity. Apparently, knowing who you really are brings comfort and consolation. Being reminded of who you really are immediately cloaks you in an identification that contradicts what you may have done. And this in itself is an act of mercy simply because you are well aware that your actions may not line up to the label. What you believe about yourself may not agree with what your Father believes about you. But who will you believe?

In the days when Jesus walked the Earth, the Pharisees—or religious elite, were puzzled when He said *"go and learn what this means: I desire mercy and not sacrifice"* (Matt 9:13 NKJV). That is to say, God is more concerned with being merciful toward us, than simply demanding sacrificial offerings from us. Don't misunderstand me here. There is absolutely something to be said of sacrificing some things to God, such as our time or our money. But we don't do these things in order to earn God's mercy toward us. We don't sacrifice our time in order to persuade God to forgive our sins.

There was a time when the sacrificing of animals pleased God. In the Old Testament God required the children of Israel to make yearly sin sacrifices in order to atone for their sins. This practice was initiated by God Himself when He slaughtered the first animal in order to cover Adam and Eve in their nakedness--shamefulness. But this process of sacrificing animals was not completely suitable to God. The real bottom line is that the sacrifice required to obliterate the original sin had to be a human sacrifice. Instead of requiring humanity to literally sacrifice themselves, God chose to **BE** the sacrifice needed in order to clear our sin accounts.

Without going off into theology, you must know that Jesus and God are one and the same. Jesus is the son of God and the express image of God Himself. Jesus was with God the Father at the beginning. Jesus is the second person in the trinity—God The Father, God The Son and God The Holy Spirit. Just as I am a mother, a daughter and a sister, God has three unique identities as well. Each has a distinct function but each is a manifestation of one God.

So in a manner of speaking, God, through the manifestation of Jesus Christ, decided to become the necessary sin sacrifice in order to save His own creation. As you grow into a deeper knowledge of God, He will grant you more insight into Who He is. This is why Jesus is so important to our stories as humans and our lives as women. He alone not only came to set the captives free, but through Jesus we have the real covering that we need. Jesus represents for us a tangible expression of God's mercy and covering grace.

You absolutely can NOT get to God without or apart from Jesus. We can talk about God ad nauseam—and I am not diminishing the importance of a sound knowledge of God—but if we fail to mention Jesus we miss the entrance into the things of God. Jesus is absolutely the *only* WAY to God. I cannot and will not let you think that by simply praying to God, apart from acknowledging Jesus, you are effecting some change in your life or even being heard by Him. Your prayers must be IN THE

NAME OF JESUS if God is going to hear them. There is a movement in this culture right now that asserts "there are many ways to God." Not so. There is only **one** WAY, and His name is Jesus. If you cannot confess that Jesus Christ is The Lord then none of the stuff that I'm talking about in this book is going to help you (if it's helping you at all . . .).

We might as well be clear on that point. I must mention Jesus because if you're going to get God's help, you need to know Jesus. You need to know that God's help comes through Jesus. And Jesus will not force Himself upon you. He needs to be invited.

God does not make impositions. He doesn't operate under a duress principle. God is not going to forcibly remove your panties because that would cause you to feel shame. And it is this specific feeling that God really dislikes—especially if someone else is causing another to feel it. Being naked with God of your own accord is one thing. But having your panties ripped off and your nakedness exposed by a third party is something else entirely. In our modern society we could call that rape or some unlawful form of sexual assault. The bible states in Proverbs: *"The king's favor is toward a wise servant, but his wrath is against him who causes shame"* (14:35 NKJV emphasis mine). God is very clear in His detest of those who cause shame. In the book of Leviticus, where the laws governing Jewish conduct are being explained, you will find verse upon verse where God is very strictly forbidding the

UNCOVERING of another's NAKEDNESS.

So why does God have such a problem with the uncovering of another's nakedness? I believe it's because He is reminded of how the enemy originally lured His creation away from Him and away from Truth. The enemy heaps hurt after hurt upon us and we in turn develop a pattern of comfort-seeking and the enemy yet pursues us with the guilt of our actions causing us to forget who we really are. Guilt has an element of shame attached to it. The enemy is unceasing in his assault against our emotions. He happens to know that when our emotions are damaged the way we relate to EVERYTHING and EVERYONE in our world will likewise be damaged.

The bible states in Proverbs 17:9, *"He who covers a transgression seeks love."* You need to know that one of the translations of the word "seek" here is: "seeks to secure." So it could be read: "He who covers a transgression seeks to secure love." This is exactly what God does, has done and continues to do for us—cover our transgressions in order that He might secure our love. It is this facet of God's character that Jesus completely embodies.

Jesus is the ultimate expression of God's love for us and His covering grace toward us. When Jesus was crucified, He became the ultimate sacrificial offering to God for the sins of humanity. This is why God necessitates that we must accept Jesus into our hearts in order to reach Him. Through Jesus, God covers our transgressions and seeks to secure our love.

That's deep y'all.

To give you a more vivid portrait of how God covers our transgressions through Jesus we need to visit the Old Testament. There is a moving story in the 9th chapter of Genesis about a man's nakedness being covered up in more ways than one. This man is Noah.   You know this guy don't you?   The Ark. The Flood.   The salvation and regeneration of humanity and animal-kind alike is because of this man.   Noah.

Perhaps Noah was a bit overwhelmed after the whole flooding-of-the-planet ordeal because the bible states that he got drunk.   We don't really know whether he was indeed overwhelmed or anything like that; the bible simply states that Noah drank some wine and became drunk.   However, the bible also states that Noah was *uncovered* —or naked—in his tent immediately following his spin of the flask.   What happens next is so crucial, but can easily be missed because of the rapidity with which it takes place in the chapter.   Just a few short verses that could easily be overlooked detail the importance of covering nakedness versus exposing it.

Verse 22 states, *"And Ham, the father of Canaan, saw the nakedness of his father and told his two brothers outside."*   **Ham** was one of Noah's three sons.   Apparently, he walked into the tent where his father was lying drunk and naked.   The bible only states that Ham then went and told his brothers.   We don't even know the manner in which he told them about their father's issue.   But what happens next marks all of these young men for the rest of their lives. The other brothers, Shem and Japheth, drape a garment over their shoulders creating a concealing barrier between the outside of the tent and their father inside of the tent. They proceed to walk into the tent backwards so as to not see their dad naked. They use the garment to cover their father's body and the bible is explicit in mentioning that even *"their faces were backward and they saw not their father's nakedness"* (Gen 9:23).

Meaning that the two young men actually turned away while they were covering Noah, and made a conscious effort not to gaze upon their dad in that state. How is it that one son just left his dad lying on the floor naked? How is it that the other sons took extreme caution in wanting to ensure their dad's dignity and comfort?

Well the outcome of this seemingly minor event was that the son who left his dad naked was cursed by his father. His dad, Noah, pronounced a curse upon Ham's entire lineage. Here's a real fun fact: the lineage of Ham includes the Canaanites and the Moabites—the people who were highly offensive to the Jews. Ruth, the woman at the well, and the woman who was called a dog by Jesus were all descended from the lineage of this son who would not cover his dad's nakedness but rather exposed it to his brothers.

This is worth a SELAH and a half. An entire nation of people was cursed because one man dishonored his father's nakedness. On the flip side of this story, the other two sons

126

were blessed by their father.   Noah spoke a blessing over their lives that ensured continual success in all of their endeavors. Perpetual and unceasing blessing was upon the households of the sons who covered their father's nakedness.   In fact, Jesus is numbered in the lineage of Shem.   There has got to be something extremely significant to God about the covering of nakedness when I consider this one brief story that affected generations and generations to come.

In all of this discourse, the big idea that you need to walk away with is this: if you are involved in any sin you are going to feel shame.   If you struggle with your identity as a Christian you are going to feel shame.   If you have a past at all, chances are, you have felt shame at some point in your life.   There is self-imposed shame, the kind that Adam and Eve felt when they became aware that they had done something wrong.   And there is people-imposed shame, the kind that the woman with issues may have felt.

In either case, the shame makes you want to hide. Shame makes you want to pull away from people, not draw near to them.   In contrast, God wants to come near to us no matter what condition we are in.   Doubled over in agonizing pain or drunk and naked in our tent.   It appears to me that God wants to be especially near to those who are too bruised by the calamities of life to come to Him.   While there are many who make their way to Him, there remain many more who need God to meet them at the well.

Are your panties on fire?   Have you quenched that fire by taking your panties off for some random man?   Do you feel the shame of either condition?   Have you had your panties stolen from you in some horrific sexual assault that left you feeling ashamed?   There is a remedy.   There is Someone you can take your panties off for and He will not make you feel ashamed.   In fact, He will supply you with a custom-made under garment suitable for any situation.   He has a fresh pair of panties for you, but you must take off the ones you have on now.

God has your panties, but you have to get them from Jesus.   Don't let shame keep you from getting what you need. Your heart is hurt.   Your soul is wounded.   Your spirit is broken.   And for years all you've wanted is answers.   All you've wanted is someone to wrap you up in his arms and tell you, "it's ok, I got you."

Being single hurts and makes you feel especially ashamed because you walk around and see every other woman with someone and you wonder, "what's wrong with me?"   Instead of believing what our Father has said about us, we forget who we really are.   We try to alleviate the pain of singleness by settling for a man who has no intention of being a husband to us.   We alleviate the pain of singleness by having sex with men we actually don't even like.

Shoot—we alleviate the pain of singleness by having sex with ourselves.   We just want to forget for a moment that we feel undesirable because we have been single for so long.   And the knowledge of all of this makes us feel ashamed. The enemy creeps into our hearing and tells us "God has forgotten about you," "you've been with too many men," "you've got too many kids for a man," "you're never getting married again." And then we pull on the panties of compromise and agree with the enemy of our souls.

And to add worst to worse, church-folk chime in and criticize you. Unwilling to just love you in your season of searching or waiting to be found, they make you feel small and isolated. Instead of being the kind of "brothers" or sisters that walk into our tents of shame and spread the covering of love, they run out of our tents like Ham and spread the word about our condition. God's got news for YOU. He has seen you at your worst and has never stopped loving you. He has not changed His mind about who He says you are. YOU are not some generic daughter. YOU are a daughter with a promise. And if you will press through the shame and find His hand He is going to comfort you like no one else can.

The grace of God is not about you maxing out your sin-credit-card by doing whatever you want to do as so many people believe. God knows what's really in your heart. His grace is about covering you as you attempt to walk toward Jesus broken and bruised by life's calamities.

The reality is that you're going to stumble until your heart is healed. You're going to bleed and bleed and bleed until you cut through the throngs of onlookers. In that place God has promised never to turn away from you. He has promised not to crush you when you're already down. Matthew 12:20 declares, *"a bruised reed He will not break, and smoking flax He will not quench (snuff out) till He sends forth justice to victory"* (NKJV). In that process of healing, even after you have given your panties to another man . . . again, God will cover you and not make you feel ashamed. YES HE WILL! But it is necessary for you to walk toward Him . . . or crawl if you need to. Get the panties that are a perfect fit every time and for every occasion. They're always in season. They won't bunch up, ride up, or be ill fitting. They will be the most comfortable and comforting pair of panties you will ever wear. And the last pair you'll ever need. Try God's GRACE on; it's one size fits ALL.

Chapter 5

Not Yo Mamma's Panties...

ou've just read the title of this chapter and right now you're wondering, "What in the world does my momma have to do with anything going on in this book?" Who you are as a woman is a direct or indirect result of the example shown to you by your mother or lack thereof. As much as this society pushes the "father in the home" agenda, no real push for mothers-in-the-home is ever discussed at length. Yes, fathers are absolutely essential to the family unit. Yet the role of mothers gets widely ignored. The truth, of course, is that children need BOTH parents. However, the reality is that there are statistically more single parent households in America than two parent households; and women usually head those households that are parented singularly. So one of the big questions to ask is: what role does a mother play in shaping her daughter's identity and femininity? Something else to consider is: how was womanhood modeled for you in the time that you were being molded into a woman? How is womanhood modeled for girls in today's culture? And what in the world does a mother-model have to do with MY PANTIES??

Of all the pages that I have written in this book, this chapter is by far the most difficult for me. Strange huh? I just told you about my sexual rampage of the very near past. I exposed critical potentially damaging information in regard to my sexuality. But ask me to talk about WHO I AM AS A WOMAN, and I'm all stops. Better yet, ask me to talk about MY MOTHER AND ME and you have successfully acquired speechlessness from this writer. Here's what you need to know: I and my mother still don't have the greatest relationship. What started off as stark absence proceeded to minimal contact and is now bruised force-fed small talk. I'm not even sure I can term it a genuine "relationship."

As the new saying goes, "it is what it is" with me and my mother. My heart wants to have a great relationship with her. But how do you have a relationship with someone you have never known? Or even someone who is still subject to injure you at any given time? Its one thing to allow the wounds of the past to scab over, but quite another to have those scabs ripped off by the very person who created them in the first place.

An ongoing assault to my feelings is what I often endure with my mother.

The guarding of my heart remains paramount when dealing with her. The desire to treat her with the honor that God commands is fleeting. While the desire to write her off completely and proceed with my own life is more than eminent. And ultimately I find myself incapable of doing either effectively. I cannot write my mom off. God commands that I honor her and respect her whether she deserves it or not. While the pain of my past where she is concerned never seems to be fully rectified, I have to yet deal with the pain of the very real present of who she is right now. And who I am because of who she was and is to me is someone who is very unsure of herself.

Unsure of who I am in relation to her and because of her—my mom. Am I a daughter? And if a daughter, why do I feel so unloved by the woman who gave me life? What do I need from her? Is there anything she can give me to make up for the years of never mothering me or showing me how to be a woman? Am I a woman? And why does all of this still affect me RIGHT NOW? Tough questions. No real answers—yet.

Since this book is largely about my unique struggles as a single Christian woman, I need to tell you a little more about how I arrived at being the woman that I am today. My mother was not around much when I was growing up. My parents were divorced early in my life and my FATHER was the custodial parent. When I was growing up, single parents were not the norm, and of the single parents that existed I don't even remember seeing one father besides mine. But alas, my dad took on the task of raising two daughters on his own. And did a stellar job if I do say so myself. He is in heaven now. Even so, because my father was my main visible parent, I missed out on a lot of female classes, such as Nurturing 101, Modern Femininity 105, and of course Relating-To-a-Man 102. I know this information presents an interesting dichotomy to you right now. I was raised by a man so relating to one should come naturally to me, right? WRONG!

Here's another bit of truth: a woman can only learn how to be woman by another woman. I am saying this in a very particular sense; there are certain feminine qualities that my father couldn't teach me. Just as there are certain masculine qualities I cannot teach my son. You want to know another very alarming truth? There is not one example in the bible of a mother-daughter relationship. I will wait while you search for one . . . . . . I know Ruth and Naomi come pretty close, and certainly we will not discount the wisdom of that story as it relates to mothers and daughters, but remember Naomi is a mother-in-law.

There is the father-son relationship a myriad of times. We can go back to Noah and his sons for ample proof of that. There is even a minute instance of a father-daughter relationship. If you search around the Old Testament in the book of Numbers you'll find proof of that. There is even still a mother-son relationship expressed in the bible. The entire last chapter of

134

Proverbs are the words of a mother to her son. But the one example we as women genuinely need to see modeled cannot even be found in the Word of God. That's stunning, if you ask me. So what do we do with that? How do we tackle this issue of raising daughters effectively, let alone finding our own feminine identity, when we can't even look to the bible, the map and guide for our lives?

I took this issue to God a long time ago. I inquired as to why there was no model of a healthy mother-daughter relationship to be found in His word. The response I received was still not very comforting. God told me, "A daughter learns how to be a woman by watching her mother as she relates to her (the daughter's) father." Great answer, right?

Well, it gets sticky when there are certain elements of the family equation that are missing, for instance, an absent father. So a daughter must look to her mother to model womanhood as the mother relates to *whom* in that particular case? We can certainly insert God our Father into this equation, but there is still going to be some lack on the part of what the daughter learns.

Please don't take this the wrong way—in no way am I saying "God You messed up." The state and condition of our modern families is a primary result of the devil's influence on the world. He has come into our homes and lives and ransacked the family unit leaving it devoid of authority figures such as fathers and mothers. And if not completely absent of them, the enemy has ensured that parents are extremely crippled in their ability to parent effectively. This by no means is the fault of God. I am simply pointing out that there are some issues we need to take to God directly because there really are some things that cannot be found in the bible.

Now, suppose we have a daughter without a mother. What does that look like? How in the world does a father model femininity? He can't. He can absolutely treat his daughter with the gentle loving touch of a father and thereby demonstrate to her how she should expect to be treated by any other man. Yet, I fully believe that there is information on being a woman that this particular father would not have. And this is the equation that many women are struggling to figure out today: daughter (minus) mother=?? Motherlessness. This was my equation.

For every deficit we can name relative to fatherlessness, I can assure you that those double when the absent parent is the mother. A woman doesn't know who she is, who she can be, or what she has when her mother is not present. When I see little girls walking to school wearing shorts that look more like underwear, I can't help but wonder, "Where is her momma?" A mother should be the one to show her daughter how to respect her body. A mother should be the one to teach her how to dress appropriately. A mother should be the first one to show her daughter what a woman is supposed to look like—because a mother should have a problem when her daughter walks out of the house half-naked. Yet many girls, even those whose mothers are present, are left to their own devices to figure out womanhood and femininity for themselves.   I was.

As a woman who had to figure out femininity on her own, I can tell you that there is much I still don't know at the age of 33.   And with this profound lack of knowledge I am supposed to raise girls of my own to be women in this 21st century.   You'll have to excuse me, because right now I need to SELAH for a few moments.

There is a story about a dog and her puppies that I will never forget.   This dog had been injured in an accident while she was pregnant.   The dog never walked the same afterwards. She walked with a very pronounced limp—to the point it appeared that she was dragging herself across the floor.   The dog eventually gave birth to a healthy litter of puppies.   But something strange happened as they grew up.   The puppies began to walk in the same manner that their mother walked by dragging themselves across the floor.

They were not injured in any way.   What they had seen their mother do—how she walked and carried herself—they simply began to mimic.   They believed that the way their mother was walking was the proper way to walk.   Their mother was the only influence they had in their little puppy lives.   She was the only visible identification that was similar in appearance to themselves.   So naturally, whatever she did they merely followed because they respected her image.   She was responsible for teaching them how to walk, how to carry

137

themselves and how to live as dogs in their world. But how could she teach them how to walk properly when she was crippled herself?

This story is sad but startling to me. How many women today are doubled over in their own pain unable and incapable of teaching their daughters how to walk upright or at least stand straight? I am such a woman. I am quite aware of my own deficits and incapacities as a mother. I am very cognizant of the fact that parenting my daughters does not come easy to me. I struggle to show my daughters affection. I struggle to nurture them adequately.

I struggle to show my girls a worthy example of womanhood and to show them how to live as women in their world. I have even struggled with identifying them as "my girls." A dear friend of mine had to point this out to me. I struggle to figure out who I really am as a woman. A mother. Even after having been a parent for the past 14 years of my life and a female all of my life—I still struggle.

My femininity has been shaped and informed by all of my experiences throughout the duration of my life, as well as the influence of my own mother, who was mostly absent. And I can tell you right now that there has been some definite misinformation given me. There has been some definite misappropriation of my personal experience. There has been some definite damage to my feminine identity. And with all of this lack I find myself oftentimes dragging my dilapidated weathered-by-life's storms body across the floor of generational gaps attempting to train up my girls in the way that they *SHOULD* go.   And that particular "way" is often elusive to me.

Why do I not know this "way" of being feminine?   Why do I not know this "way" of being a woman?   Because the "way" that was supposed to be shown to me, was not.   Because the "way" that was supposed to be mapped out for me, was not. The way of womanhood, for THIS woman, was strewn with ambiguities and empty spaces—particularly one gigantic empty space where a mother should have been.   And how does this fact relate to my panties?   Without the proper information on how to perceive myself as a woman and then relate to a man, I was forced to trust hearsay.

I was forced to trust "my gut."   I was forced to trust what I had seen in movies and on television.   I was forced to trust the experiences of other women in my life that I had the unfortunate displeasure of witnessing while they related to men. In a nutshell, I had to "wing it" when it came to being a woman or a girl or a feminine BE-ing.   I had to trust the misinformation of others and my ill-informed SELF.   A woman with no knowledge of womanhood in a world where the image of womanhood is slightly distorted and skewed at best—is where I AM right now.   Add all of this to the fact that I am presently raising daughters who are becoming women as well and you have quite a sticky situation indeed.

One thing I have witnessed in regard to daughters and

their mothers is this: as a woman you will either RESPECT the image of your mother or REJECT the image of her. And this goes for good qualities as well as unsavory. If my mother was loving toward me but hurtful toward men and other people, I would respect her example and mimic her behavior by likewise treating men with contempt.

In contrast, if my mother was unloving toward me yet cordial and becoming to everyone else, I would reject her example of goodness simply to maintain the notion "I don't want to be like her." This may not be the absolute truth for every situation. Certainly there are people who rise above the influence of their parents whether negative or positive, as we all should strive to do. There are even those who mimic the mistreatment that they were the victim of. In any case, I'm merely speaking my opinion and discussing things I have noticed in my 32 years of living. However, I cannot deny that each one of us is a product of our parents influence in many ways.

Suppose "Sally's" mother was a great loving wife who honored her husband. If Sally felt ill treated by her mother, she may grow up disrespecting men in an effort to disrespect the image of her mom. I've seen it all too often. Shoot—I'm living it as I write. Not that I disrespect men, but the relationships that I have had with them have suffered because of the relationship I had and have with my mom. How so, you ask? Because how I identify myself as a woman is based on the relationship I have and had with my mom. For so many women in the world today, society would love to blame absent fathers for faulty female-male relationships, but I must disagree with that notion to an extent. Not having a good relationship with my mother has left me with a feeling of discontent and confusion as to who I am as a woman.

Not knowing who I am as a woman causes me to enter relationships with men in order to find out who I am. Because when you don't know who you are, you'll look to others to tell you who you are. What I believe about myself is largely based on what I hear about myself—either in action or word, and I believe this is true for every one of us.

One of the most important voices that speak into my belief of who I am is my mother. By all accounts she should be. But what happens when what is spoken is hurtful, cruel or even missing? Here's what I am basically trying to say: I am a sum total of the influence of my mother and other women who were a part of my life as a child. My father's solution to his inability to teach me femininity was to leave me in the hands of women he thought more apt to do so while I was blossoming into a young lady.

While my mother was absent, the women who could have offered some feminine guidance were not interested in doing so. What I didn't know at the time was that these women were crippled themselves and incapable of filling in the gaps that my mother had left. Therefore, the lack of affection and extreme lack of affirmation towards me didn't just come from my mother, but from grandmothers, aunties and many other older women with the position of caregiver in my life. All of these women had direct influence over me as a girl. And the influence of women in maternal roles on girls is crucial to the development of femininity and self-identity.

I was not taught how to care for myself during my menstruation—I had to figure that one out on my own. I was not taught how to shave my legs—actually, my father taught me that. I was not taught how to appreciate being a girl. So what was my image of woman? Being tough. Being a no-nonsense-sharp-tongued "ride or die chick." Being a "strong Black woman" who never lets a man get the upper hand. My image of woman had more to do with "winning" than anything else. That is, as long as I am smarter than a man, make more money than a man, or have more things "going for myself" than a man then, consequently, I WIN. Now, I had no idea what I had theoretically "won," but this is what was patterned for me as a girl.

This is how I watched the women in my life identify themselves and deal with men. Deep down I knew that something was wrong with these ideas, but I had no clue as to what it was at that time in my life. All I knew is that I didn't want to be like them; and I tried with all my might not to be. In essence, I rejected their image of woman and tried as best as I could to be the opposite of what I saw. Where they were hard and uncompromising; I was trying to be extra compromising and soft. In so doing, I actually rejected some valuable life lessons I could have garnered from them.

The maternal women in my life were indeed tough. They were no-nonsense strong Black women—a trait to be honored and respected when properly balanced with femininity and godliness. Yet, because I felt so maltreated by them I not only rejected what I thought was an unworthy example of womanhood, but I also rejected the things that could have been of benefit to me in the overall scope of living. I watched these women endure life in the south where racism and prejudice have reigned for centuries and rise above the angst.

I watched them live the best life that they could among the thorns and snares of their own bruised past. I also watched as they gave to me whatever they could in terms of a sense of self. But my heart had been so bruised by them that I would not receive from them and could not perceive any good from them either. When I was growing up they were just mean-old-women. As a woman myself now looking back I can see that they were limping through life just as I am now.

In addition to the toxicity of non-feminine female role models, as I mentioned earlier I also had grand old TELL-A-VISION. And it was most definitely telling me a vision of who I should be. It presented a constant assault on my self-image and self-esteem and self-confidence with its images of perfectly sculpted flawless women. Not having my mother around to show me and teach me how to conduct myself as a lady and feel good about who I was at the time left me watching popular television programs when I was growing up

143

and admiring the women I saw. The admiration led to respect and then respect led to a copying of behavior. I'm sure we've all heard the phrase "imitation is the greatest form of flattery," and truly it is. What you respect you will eventually practice. And practice really does make perfect. When a person practices self-control, she will eventually perfect that character trait.

The same principle holds true in the negative also. If a person practices lying, she will eventually perfect *that* character trait as well. This is why we have to be careful of what we admire. We must be conscious of certain character traits that we deem laudable. When we admire characteristics that are unpleasant, we make it easy to mimic unpleasantness ourselves. This is one main reason why parents must monitor what their children are taking in and model appropriate behavior. Even this principle can be difficult to practice because that forces us as parents to monitor what WE ourselves are taking in. Go ahead and SELAH.

The bible says in 1 Corinthians 15:33, *"Be not deceived, evil communications corrupt good manners."* Many of us have heard this verse read "bad company corrupts good character." While certainly the company one keeps factors in to this truth, the express meaning intended here is deeper than simply "keeping company" with someone. In this verse, "communications" refers to the act of communing with something or someone. The implication is that a genuine influence over another's character must take place. And this happens by spending quality time with whomever or whatever the "company" is. For instance, if we commune with God, we are not simply just keeping company with God. We are intimately spending quality time with Him and allowing His presence to influence us—to saturate us. And a person can COMMUNE with just about anything—to include television, the radio, the internet just to name a few. That is the danger.

The last word in this verse, "manners," is the Greek word ETHOS—where we get our term "ethics" from. Our ETHOS has to do with our perceptions of right and wrong. When we lose our ability to tell right from wrong we are in dire straits indeed, and truly our "character" is what lies in the balance. When studying this verse, I found the translations for "evil" quite interesting. One of them was, "Not such as it ought to be," in other words, contrary. If I Dreanify this verse it would read: "Spending quality time with that which is contrary corrupts your capacity to tell right from wrong." Things that make you go hhmm.

There I was, growing up in an environment where what I saw was *contrary* to what I should be. What I heard was *contrary* to what I should be. And the things I heard and saw were framing an alternate identity for me. Television became a voice whispering into my identity as I communed with it daily. Older women that I kept *company* with became a voice whispering into my identity. And because I did not have a sound image of myself that was forged by the words and actions of my mother, it was easy for me to believe whatever I heard and saw.

When God says, *"Faith comes by hearing. . ."* in 1 Corinthians 33:15, I think that applies to more than just faith in God. Faith or confidence in yourself comes by hearing. Faith or confidence in another person can also come by hearing. Our faith, whether for good or bad, comes by what we hear about a thing. In other words, what I hear is what I will believe in and ultimately what I will become. The bible states in Proverbs 23:7, *"For as he (a man) thinks in his heart so is he."* Thinking and believing go hand-in-hand. What you think is what you become, and what you believe and accept as true—agree with—will manifest.

The principle of agreement outlined in Matthew 18:19 works no matter what you agree to. If you agree with God's word then godliness will manifest. If you agree to things that are contradictory to God's word then those will likewise manifest. Not only will what you agree to and believe in manifest, but also what you respect because what you believe in and agree to you also respect by default. As a young lady, I was learning to respect, believe in and agree to things that were not healthy for my identity as a woman. Many of the things I heard and saw were hurtful and damaging to my self-identity. And many times, the things I heard and saw were not necessarily hurtful; they were merely *contrary* to my best self.

Here is something else I have learned: when you don't know who you are you will rely on the words of others to frame your own self-image. This can actually be a good thing in cases where what is heard is something edifying. However, more often than not it is detrimental to our self-perception when the words we hear contradict how we should perceive ourselves. As children grow up they need to hear that they are doing a good job, or that they are handsome or beautiful—they need to be affirmed.

This promotes a healthy self-image, and there is nothing wrong with a sound self-image. Even God knows the importance of affirmation. Jesus Himself didn't begin His ministry until He heard the affirming words of His Father, "*This is my beloved Son in Whom I am well pleased*" (Matthew 3:17). Still wonder if God approves of our need to be affirmed?

Its one thing to bolster a child's self-image; and it's quite another to ignore reality and over indulge in verbal praise. For example, it would not be promoting a healthy self-image if a parent were to ignore the misbehavior of their child and continue to praise him instead of correcting him. Parents are pivotal in promoting appropriate self-identities in their children, and it all starts with what they hear and what they see.

With all the talk about SELF I do not want to make the impression that we should be entirely SELF aware and SELF conscious. There is something to be said of identifying yourself in a right and ordinate manner. Yet there is much to be said of taking this idea to extremes and being completely self-indulged. The latter is just as detrimental to our spiritual health as growing up with a tainted self-image. In the ultimate end the goal ought to be to see ourselves the way God intends for us to, and at the same time grow our confidence in Him and not rely on our own SELF-confidence. The danger in doing that—being self-confident—is that we will look to ourselves to meet our needs. We will look to ourselves to find the answers we seek. We will look to ourselves and believe that WE are all we need in life—not Jesus.

And to do this is an affront to God. We basically tell God that we can take care of ourselves without His intervention and assistance. And that is the biggest lie the world has ever told. Yes—we should absolutely feel good about who we are, but we should feel good about WHOSE we are as well; who God has made us to be through Jesus.

In our society today there is a movement of SELFism that is really unhealthy. As much as we want to believe in ourselves and believe the best for ourselves, the world wants to push God's people into a distorted frame of mind where the only thing that matters in life is YOU. Don't get me wrong—you absolutely matter. But you matter TO GOD, not just to yourself. You matter to the world in which you live. You sincerely and honestly matter, but you must have the right scale to balance how much you matter and to whom.

As a woman raising woman-children in a cold cruel world, I cannot afford to teach my daughters that the only one who matters in their life is their SELF. I have experienced too much selfishness. Even while my own feminine identity and self-identity are bruised, I refuse to perpetuate in them the gross selfism that I was a victim of.

In the overall scheme of things, I had a misfortunate upbringing in regard to learning how to be a woman. I still feel the effects of that upbringing today. The fight, for me, is to get through all the junk of wrong words spoken and contrary models presented and figure out who I am right now and who God wants me to be in my future. When our lives have been ill-informed our self-perception is tainted and from that tainted place we view our world and attempt to relate to it. And it is near impossible to relate to anything or anyone appropriately with a cloudy self-perception.

If you can't view yourself right, then you certainly can't view anyone or anything else right either, to include God. We attempt to relate to men as well as other women with this faulty self-perception that was fed to us. That misshapen identity grows and disfigures our reality and renders us strangers in the land of femininity. The art of being a woman is then lost because we did not have a sound model to begin with. The good news is that God made woman. He knows what real femininity should look like, sound like and be like. The model might have been flawed, but The Maker is not.

Yes—our mothers are partly responsible for who we are at this very moment. It is OK to acknowledge that. However, we have to forgive her. I have had and STILL have to forgive my mother. She has her own share of a faulty upbringing that I am certain I am not completely aware of. I can't fault her for that. I can't continue to blame my mom or other women who were in my life that I thought SHOULD HAVE taught me something along the lines of being a woman. They had their own flawed models of femininity. The real culprit guilty of our misshapen identities is the devil, just as he was the real culprit in The Garden Of Eden.

The devil is the reason for contrariness that exists in the world today. Not our moms. The devil is the reason women don't know what being a woman really looks like. It is not our fault that we may not know, but that doesn't mean we cannot learn. Is it right to fault our mothers for what they didn't know and were incapable of teaching us? We want to—and oftentimes, we do because it's not fair. It's not right.

For many of us, we are living a life handed to us and have no knowledge about how to live it to the best of our ability. Being a woman is as foreign to many of us as being on another planet. And God knows that. God is not unaware of the fight I had to engage in for my identity; and He is not unaware of your fight either. He is not unaware that we are still fighting today. This is why He says, *"FIGHT the good fight of FAITH. . ."* (1 Timothy 6:12).

What Paul is saying to us all in this verse is that we must fight to believe. We must fight to believe the right things about ourselves and our mothers. We must fight to believe the right things about one another and even God. We must fight to believe that we are not just the sum of the isolated parts of our fractured past. In that same verse, Paul goes on to say that we must "take hold of the eternal *life* to which you were called." This means that there is a life that God has called us to. There is a life that God has designated and planned for us—but we have to fight for it.

We have to fight through the death that was spoken to us, the death that we witnessed from having a flawed model of femininity, and the death that we manifested out of our own wrong companionships (bad company). We have to fight through the death so that we can in turn take hold of life. Our real lives. The lives God intends for us to live. And the fight is grueling. It's tiring. It's frustrating. It seems like there's no end. But God has promised that WE WIN!

2 Corinthians 2:14 declares, *"Now thanks be unto God, which ALWAYS causes us to TRIUMPH* (emphasis mine). YOU win—ALWAYS! No matter the fight. No matter the foe. YOU WILL ALWAYS WIN! Yo' momma might have done you wrong. You might not have even had a momma. Fight to believe that God will make it right. You feel like a failure at relationships with other women. Fight to believe that God will bring you into friendships that will bless your life. You feel like you can't win with men. Fight to believe that your identity is not tied to the man in your life. You feel like you don't know how to be a woman. Fight to believe that God will show you. He says, *"Call to Me and I WILL answer you, and I will tell you great and mighty things which YOU DO NOT*

KNOW" (Jeremiah 33:3 NASB emphasis mine). Whatever YOU DO NOT KNOW, fight to believe that God can teach you Himself. A fight is not a fight if you don't show up. So take off your shoes, pull back your hair, put on your panties and FIGHT LIKE A GIRL! Your LIFE really is on the line—the life that God has prepared for you.

Chapter 6

Cleaning out the panty drawer

I'm not sure how you're feeling about all that I've said thus far, but there is a point—I promise. In the last chapter I had to divulge some things about my life that I am really not comfortable with discussing. Another pair of panties had to come off. This process of stripping away and facing the music does not end. It goes on and on until we have nothing left to expose. And to be quite honest, I'm not sure there will ever be anything unworthy of exposure in our lives. I believe that there will always be something requisite of the Son's light. I had to go there with the issues of me and my mother because I know that is a big part of who I am right now. I know that how I relate to myself, other women and certainly men is all tied to what has happened between my mom and me.

And the biggest part of all of this is that I must recognize it for what it is. I must deal with the WHOLE truth about who I am. I must look into the panty drawer of my past, sift through the junk, keep the necessities, and dispense with what no longer has use. But all in all, rummaging through the drawers of my life serves an even greater purpose than merely coming to grips with it. It allows me to see where I am, how far I've come and where I need to be.

Earlier this year I embarked on a "purging" mission. You might as well know this: I can be a bit of a "hoarder" at times. I'm a single parent and things have a tendency to pile up. School papers on desks. Bills on counter tops. Folded laundry needing to be put away. I don't always have the time or energy to devote to maintaining complete and utter order in my home—particularly my closet. So one day I decided to attack it.

As I was looking through boxes and file bins I was astounded by the age of some of the things that I had kept. When I had finished for the day (because this endeavor literally took several days) I looked at the pile of un-useful rubbish, sat on my bed and began to weep. I wept sorely too. I realized that I had allowed so much STUFF to accumulate in my life that the necessities were being crowded out. I realized that I was responsible for this mess; the devil hadn't come to my room and forced me to keep this or that. I had grown tired. I had gotten weary. I had just grown a little lethargic and languid and no longer bothered to do the work of keeping useful things and discarding unnecessary things—synthesizing my life, maintaining order and balance.

When we are overcome with pain, that fact alone can cause paralysis. Not only had I grown tired from life in general, but I was also in extreme emotional turmoil. Cleaning my closets was the furthest thing from my mind. I just wanted to feel better. I just wanted to NOT hurt anymore. So I ignored life. I ignored small things that required my attention—putting away folded laundry.

I ignored big things that required my attention—reading through my children's school papers. I was living, but barely. Alive, but not really. I was existing; present but only physically. Pain can do this to you. Grief can do this to you. It can make you neglect the things that you genuinely need to do because you're tending to wounds. Or at least you think you are, because "tending to wounds" isn't necessarily an active thing. It usually looks more like just sitting and wondering WHY.

Then of course there is the constant reevaluation and reassessment of all the events that have taken place—rehearsal. At least, this is how I thought I was tending to *my* wounds. Blind to everything else going on around me—to include my children and even myself—I would sit in my room and think. And think...and think about how much that guy hurt me; and

155

not just that guy, but *any* guy who has ever hurt me—any *person* who has ever hurt me.   And since I couldn't come up with any legitimate reasons WHY that one particular guy, or anyone else for that matter, could be so cruel to me I just made some up. Or better stated, I tuned in to old voices that had once told me I was not good enough for anyone, I was not beautiful enough, I was not spiritual enough, I was not sexy enough, I was not Black enough; I was just NOT ENOUGH.   In that place life was moving past me.   Life was crowding me out.   Pain was all I could feel and accumulated STUFF was all that I could see.

How did I get out?   Well, truthfully I'm still kind of there.   The extreme pain has subsided.   But there is still pain. Real pain doesn't let up easily.   I'm in a far better place than I was a year ago, but honestly I'm still in a bit of pain.   Yeah—I know, not what you expected huh?   You were expecting this mighty shout of jubilee and victory because *SURELY* after having written this book I must now be "over it," and walking in my place of divine-overcomer-ness.

Well, as you can clearly see by now, I value the absolute uncut TRUTH.   And THAT is this: While I am certainly in a better place than I was at the onset of this book, I have discovered that healing is a process and not always an event. There are things that God can absolutely do for us in an instant. Yet, there are some things He will walk us THROUGH.   And I still got my hiking boots on.   The work of undoing decades of wounds has definitely begun.   But it is in no way complete yet. I am thankful that I am learning again how to live.   I am

156

learning how to love for real.   I am learning that it takes time to heal completely FOR REAL.

When I was going through this tumultuous time of emotional torment, God showed me an image of how healing really takes place.   He gave me a vision of someone with a broken leg.   The initial pain for that person was unbearable. However, instead of properly tending to the broken leg and allowing it to heal correctly, the person proceeded to do things normally as if she wasn't hurt.   Well, not long after the original injury the person hurt herself again—same spot, same type of injury.   The problem this time is that the secondary injury was exacerbating the original one.

Because the person never really healed from the first injury, the second injury had taken her down for the count. Here is the gruesome part: in order for the secondary injury to heal at all, a re-creation of the original injury had to take place; the leg had to be re-broken.   A qualified strategic surgeon had to go deep inside the injured spot and take a good look at what the real problem was.   The healing process after such a prolonged perpetual injury would be long and painful.   But in the end the injured leg would have been saved and would be stronger and able to bear-up under normal pressure.

The owner of the leg would be able to enjoy complete restoration of her leg.   Then again, maybe not necessarily "complete restoration" because in the ultimate end she just might walk a little different as evidence of extreme prior injury.

This was me.   Except it wasn't my leg that was broken; it was my heart.   And I got a hunch that it may very well be many of you too—limping around with broken wounded hearts pretending you are healed when in reality you are not.

The pain that I thought was from a simple break-up was actually much deeper than that.   God had to lay me flat on my back and show me what the condition and real issues of my heart were.   You see, when I reconnected with "old friend" that incident was not the trap that the enemy had prepared for me. The real trap that the devil had set-up for me was prepared well before I was an adult, even before I was an adolescent.   This particular trap was initiated when I was a little girl feeling unloved by mother.

Feeling rejected by my peers.   Feeling invisible in my world.   This was the pain and woundedness that had never healed.   This was the place I was immediately reminded of when "old friend" rejected me.   The enemy ensured that I would parallel my already shaky view of myself with the events surrounding this new injury to my heart.   And it worked.

Looking around at my messy drawers and closets I realized I was in more pain than I had originally thought.   I also realized that I had not healed properly from old wounds.   I pulled on a pair of self-made panties and did my best to cope with life.   I did my best to limp along through smiles and hugs trying to prove to myself that I was OK.   But I was not.   I was bleeding-out all over the place. Evidence of woundedness showed up in the way I treated my kids, the way I cared for myself and even the way I maintained my home. My closet was just an outside reflection of what was going on inside of me. A MESS—and one that I had been ignoring for many years.

It would be ridiculous and cruel for anyone to expect a person who broke his leg yesterday to get up and walk the way that he used to. No. That person needs REST, for one thing. Then he needs therapy. And even in the midst of therapy he needs more rest. Finally, after the rest and the therapy, the recuperating person needs practice. That person must learn to live and function with their rehabilitated leg. Some days the pain may not be as intense as other days. Some days there may be no pain at all. But every day that person will have to celebrate a small victory.

Every day that injured leg will get better and better. But it is certainly a day-by-day effort. Heart injuries are no different. In fact, I would argue that heart injuries are more severe. It is the heart that guides our belief system, as I've already discussed earlier. Broken injured heart=haywire belief system. And when a person's belief system is tad bit off, the way she functions in life is significantly more than "a tad bit off." Think about a ship plotting a course through a large body of water. If that ship's navigation system is off by just a hair of a degree it could potentially be lost at sea. That's life with a broken heart.

Heart in pieces trying to function in everyday normal life

was where I had found myself not too long ago. And functioning "normal" was proving to be intensely arduous for me. In my healing process God had to take me back to where it all started. He had to show me the original wounds. He had to let me see where the hurts had come from. Certainly, that guy had hurt me, but his one hurt was just the hair on the scale that caused a major tilt.

I was reminded of the story in the bible about a man chopping some wood. This guy was doing what he normally did with an axe and then the head of his axe flew off. Not only did it fly off, it went into the river and sank (2 Kings 6). In just two verses the issue is resolved. So it seems rather insignificant then, the axe head and its recovery. The bible doesn't even give this guy a name. But we know about his axe. A tool used to cut things down.

A tool used to turn one thing into something else of better use. An axe. And the most useful part of the tool sank to the bottom of a body of water. I find the most interesting part of the whole story to be the fact that the man cutting the wood requested the presence of the man of God—the prophet Elisha. Why is that? That's what we should be focused on. For so many years I have heard an interpretation that only focuses on the axe and its recovery, which is certainly of extreme import. But I think the real focus ought to be on the prophet and his proximity to the problem. Why was Elisha there anyway?

In chapter 6 of 2nd Kings the very first verse is about moving on. Some men—simply called "the sons of the prophets"—come to Elisha, who is the appointed prophet over the children of Israel. They tell him something along the lines of: "This town isn't big enough for the both of us!" Now, they were in no means being antagonistic toward the man of God or expressing anger. They were simply acknowledging their need to move to a place where there was room for them to dwell comfortably.

Interestingly, they want to build a habitation at Jordan. What is significant about this particular body of water is that in the previous chapter a dignitary, Naaman, had been healed by bathing in the Jordan River at the demand of this same prophet, Elisha, who accompanies these young men. That doesn't sound too odd. Here is the glitch: Naaman considered the Jordan not dignified enough for him to bathe in. The Jordan River was not the cleanest and probably not the most beautiful looking river. But Elisha told the man to go and bathe in the Jordan River to be healed. Flash forward to the very next chapter following this story, and "the sons of the prophets" have decided to live near this same river.

But I must ask again: Why was Elisha there? There is no reason given other than he was asked by the men and he agreed to go with them. These men were "sons of the prophets," so we can assume that they knew God. And while they are in pursuit of a better life they wanted the man of God near. Perhaps they wanted Elisha to bless their new home.

Or maybe they wanted to ensure their safety by having a prophet with them who was known to have God's presence with him. No explanation is given regarding why they asked Elisha to join them.   But he was with them.

I have no doubt that they had witnessed the miracles performed through Elisha.   I have no doubt that they were well acquainted with God's saving power that translates into a knowledge of divine protection.   I believe they simply felt safe knowing that God's representative was near; because if he was near then God Himself was also near.

Something you need to be aware of is that the word "Jordan" means "descending."   I promise I'm taking you somewhere with this—just keep tracking with me.   So what's really going on here?   We have a group of men wanting to branch out on their own.   These men are going to a new place and starting a new life; they are essentially "moving forward." However, they have to DESCEND, or go back, in order to do so. And in this process of starting over they knew that at the very least they needed God's presence with them, so they asked the man of God to go with them.   Descending to a new place in order to start a new life—or going back in order to begin again—is what these men were doing, all while recognizing their need for God's presence.   (You already know what I'm going to say—SELAH on that).

Here's where the story gets a little…muddy.   The bible states: *"But as one was cutting down a tree, the iron (axe head) fell into the water and he cried 'Alas master! For it was borrowed'"* (2 Kings 6:5 NKJV). While working to build this new life someone's axe head flies into the river—the Jordan River; the same dirty river that the dignitary didn't want to bathe in. Could the man have retrieved the axe head himself? I think so. But he didn't. It seems rather easy to me that the person who lost the axe head could have just gone into the water himself to get it. So why didn't he?

Did he have the same estimation of the river's cleanliness that Naaman had? Or perhaps the water was murky and he could not see where the iron had actually landed. Then again, maybe the axe head landed in a deep area of the river. Whatever the case may be, this guy, who was willing to "descend" to start a new life, is now unwilling to SUBMERGE into the river to retrieve what he needed to continue his pursuit. Interesting.

Had Elisha, a representation of God's presence, not been there, how would this man have continued moving forward? What can you do with an axe handle? It would have been a little more than difficult to build a new habitation without a tool to cut down the wood needed. In fact, losing the axe head is akin to being *un-useful*. A man needs to rebuild his future and he now finds himself ill equipped to do so. But truthfully, he was ill equipped before he went to Jordan. You see, his axe was *borrowed*. After studying the term "borrowed," as it is used here, I found that it actually indicates that this man worked really hard to obtain the axe. He didn't simply ask someone for an axe and the person supplied it to him; he had begged someone for an axe.   Sounds like a man in desperation to me.

Desperate to leave his former life with the prospect of starting a new one, having worked so hard to obtain the tools to start a new life, and now probably afraid to tell the owner that he lost what had been cautiously loaned to him—this guy is feeling some pressure.   He is now feeling un-useful and needs help. And what he needs is in a river that he doesn't want to touch. Why?

I understand that pressure.   Having come so far in life and wanting to continue for the sake of my family—just wanting to move on.   But then losing what is necessary for me to continue—my sense of usefulness.   Being rejected and having a broken heart can sure make you feel useless.   Trying to function in life with a broken heart is no less awkward than trying to cut down a tree with the handle of an axe.

When Elisha decides to help this man recover his usefulness, the implication is that God Himself steps into the situation.   After he cried out for help, the man of God asked him, *"Where did it fall?   And he (man missing axe) showed him (Elisha) the place"* (2Kings 6:6).   You see, God needs to know where the pain is coming from.   However, He also needs YOU to know where the pain is coming from.   The man only knew where the axe head had entered the river.   And like this man, we may only know that we are lost.   We may only know that something happened that left us groping around in the world without all the tools we need in order to build our lives so that we may be *useful*.

If we think about the action of chopping wood we can reasonably assume that this guy might not have seen where the axe head actually entered the river; he may have only heard it splash. Elisha only needed a general whereabouts of the axe head to offer assistance. That's all God needs; a general vicinity. "I left my panties with random man X, Y and Z..." "I am still hurting over the issues of my childhood..." "I feel lost because I'm lonely..." "I feel un-useful because I'm a single parent with no prospects of companionship..." All of these give God something to work with.

Having been shown the general whereabouts of the axe head, Elisha proceeds to intervene. The bible reads, *"He cut down a stick, and cast it tither and the iron did swim"* (2 Kings 6:6). That buried issue had to rise to the surface once God stepped into the situation. What the man needed to keep moving forward had to rise to the surface once God stepped in. What the man could not recognize before became visibly clear once God stepped in. Not only did the axe head float to the surface, but it began to SWIM. That's important to notice. The solid iron began to swim. That means that the axe head began to move toward its owner. When God uncovers the issues we have not dealt with, He brings them into full view.

So what now? The iron swims across the river toward the man, he picks it up and that's the end, right? WRONG.

Because those aren't necessarily the details.   The bible is explicit in its description of how the man picks up his axe head.   First of all, Elisha has to tell him, *"Pick it up for yourself"* (2 Kings 6:7 NKJV).   Now, if the other half of my necessary tool is SWIMMING toward me, I'm not going to wait to be told to get it.   Maybe this guy is astonished at the sight of iron doing the breaststroke in the river—I don't know.

But Elisha has to command him to pick up his tool for HIMSELF.   But wait—it gets better.   The bible could have said "and so the man picked up the axe head."   Instead, the bible reads, "So he *reached out* his hand and took it."   Sounds like a man attempting to avoid the water, if you ask me.   A person simply picking up an item does that—picks it up.   In contrast, a person reaching out is gesturing purposefully—so what's the purpose?

If we take into account all that we know about the Jordan River along with all that we have learned about this man it is not unreasonable to conclude that he may not have wanted to touch the water.   The fact that he had to be prompted by Elisha is evidence enough for me.   Here's why: when I had purposed to purge my closet I realized that it was a task that only I could do. Only I know what I still have need of, what needs to be thrown away or what needs to be organized.   No one else could do that for me.   It was my mess to sift through.   Certainly someone could have assisted me, but she wouldn't have known what was useful to me and what was not.   In like manner, the guy who lost his axe had to touch the water in order to get his own tool.

Only he could get it from the river. While God was present to reveal what had been lost, ultimately the man had to reach his own hand into the murky waters of the river that he may not have been too fond of.

Like the man in the story, I had a vague idea of where I lost my usefulness. But in no way could I go all the way down into to the murky waters of my past and recover what I had lost. NO. I needed help. I needed someone who could see through the haze of my past and present and uncover that which I couldn't see; make it known to me, bring those things in full view. Once in my view, they were my responsibility to pick up. I had to recognize them for what they were and touch the waters of my past in order to move forward.

I asked earlier: Why was Elisha with the men who were moving forward? Because God will not allow you to take another step without Him. When God is with you, even when you think you are getting away from Him, He will be right there every step of the way. I don't need to tell you the story of Jonah. God knows what we don't know—He knows that we need Him. And so He avails Himself. The "sons of the prophets" asked for God's presence to go with them as they started a new life, and He not only went with them but saved them from stagnation. Here's a fun fact: Elisha's name means "God is salvation." I'm sure those men knew that. Wanting to enlarge their territory, they knew they couldn't do a thing without God's salvation.

167

Sifting through my overcrowded closet taught me that I needed some salvation too.   Like those men, I had to go back in order to move forward.   I am still moving right now.   God had to cause my axe head to float to the surface and swim across the muddy, murky, messy river of my past.   And I had to pick it up for myself.   I had to pick up the rejection I felt from my mother. I had to pick up the rejection I felt from "old friend."   I had to pick up the lies of the enemy associated with all of those things. I had to see them for what they were—tools to help build my future.

I am not those awful things that happened to me.   But they are tools in my hands.   They serve me.   I do not serve them.   An axe may not seem to be a compatible analogy for past wounds, but it's all in how you use them.   Those things were sharp and cutting.   But they are a necessary tool useful in cutting through the forest of my present, shaping the tree of my life.   Cutting here, pruning there, ever causing me to keep forging this path that God has laid before me.

Are you your axe?   Or are you using your axe for its designated purpose?   And that is, to clear away a new path and move forward.   Whether you are clearing a path through a forest, cleaning out an overstuffed closet or cleaning out a panty drawer, the bottom line is that you have to look at things that you may have forgotten about, things you may not have known were even there.   You have to see those things for yourself and judge their usefulness, their purpose as they relate to where you are right now and where you are going.   Some things will be discarded. Others may still be of necessity. And God may have to uncover even more things in your life. When He does, will you pick them up and use them? Or will you try to avoid them? An axe can hurt you if it is held from the wrong end. An axe can serve you when it is used properly. So I ask again: are you your axe? Or is your axe sitting in the panty drawer?

Chapter 7

The Great Panty Exchange

*A*lright, I think it's time for a bit of comedy relief. Let me tell you one last story. I recently threw away a pair of panties that I have had for over a DECADE. Go ahead: gasp, grimace, shake your head, tsk and all that stuff to show your extreme disapproval. But hey—I LOVED those panties!! Seriously. They were such a good fit! They hugged my booty in all the right places. They were made from one seamless piece of fabric; *they just don't make 'em that way anymore.* They never bunched and gathered in that particular place of discomfort for us ladies. They were—in a word—perfect. They weren't the least bit stylish or ornate. They were just *soo dang comfortable.* Had they not been ruined in a drive-by bleaching accident I would STILL own those panties; you better believe I would—with pride too.

I remember looking at those panties and thinking of all the things we had been through together. These were certainly not the type I would leave with a man. They were the *private selection* type that one only wanted to wear when no one else was going to see. We ALL have a few pair of *those* panties I'm sure. Imagine my heartbreak at the prospect of trying to replace those panties. Impossible. What I learned from my ancient panty ordeal is this: even the things that we think are good to us and for us are still subject to wearing out over time. And when they do, it's OK to replace them. In fact, it's necessary to do so.

My panties had served me well over the years. They had never hurt me in any way. They were a comfortable companion. So when they needed to be discarded I had to search long and hard for a comparable replacement. Let me tell you right now: this was no easy task. I had to sift through hundreds (OK maybe not "hundreds" but certainly a significant number) of panties interrogating the quality with my fingers. Stretching here. Pulling there.

This was serious business; we're talking about the next pair of panties to don my derriere.   Trust me—I had learned my lesson with panties that were not up-to-snuff.   Now, don't get me wrong, I'm not above the multi-pack; I own several good pairs of reputable multi-pack panties.   But every now and then a woman has got to have a pair of panties that are…well, *Womanly*.   I'm happy to report that I now have a new favorite pair of panties, a few in fact.   The trouble, of course, was letting go of the old pair.   I had grown so attached to them.   I sincerely tried to salvage them, but they could not be mended. Their ultimate end was the garbage can.

In like manner, I have learned that I have to dispense with other things that are not necessarily as concrete as a pair of panties or even certain relationships, but rather certain ways of thinking, and certain ways of being.   Paul said *"when I was a child I spoke as a child, I understood as a child and I thought as a child, but when I became a man (adult) I put away childish things"* (1 Corinthians 13:11).   Interestingly, the term "put away" in this verse is actually translated DESTROYED.

In other words, Paul is saying that there came a time for him to completely do away with the part of his nature that was no longer necessary or useful to him as an adult—childish.   Of particular interest to me in this verse are the things that Paul identifies as "childish."   None of them are tangibles; none of them are things one can see.   They are all things that are internal and mental—soulish (relating to our soul).   Speaking, understanding and thinking can all have a childish connotation.

And all of these, when they are identified as childish, must be destroyed.   Think about that for a spell.

What you need to know about Paul is that he was a traditional Hebrew man.   Meaning, he knew all of the traditional practices of Jewish people and followed those to a "T." This includes the passage of young men into adulthood—the ceremony known as Bar Mitzvah.   This Jewish rite of passage is most likely what Paul was alluding to in the above scripture. While today Jewish people have a celebration to mark this event, during the time of Paul that was not the case.   Bar Mitzvah was more of a common cultural understanding than a ceremony.

Upon turning 13 years old, young men were titled "Bar Mitzvah," meaning "son of commandment," and seen in the eyes of the community as responsible adults in terms of their actions and knowledge.   They were expected to know their *history* (where they came from), as well as their *future* (who they would become).   They also had to learn how a man was supposed to conduct himself in life by being in close proximity to their fathers.   These young men had to learn their father's trade or profession by accompanying him at work.

It was at this particular stage of life that a young Jesus, traveling with His parents, was assumed lost.   Mary and Joseph had been looking for Jesus throughout Jerusalem for days. When they found Him in a temple, He said, *"How is it that you (were looking for) me?   Didn't you know that I must be about my*

Father's business?" (Luke 2:49 WEB emphasis mine). Jesus was 12 years old at this time and nearing His Bar Mitzvah. He was learning His Father's trade.

Conversely, there was no coming of age ceremony for girls during the time period covered in the bible. So what were the markers of a female's transition into adulthood? How were girls supposed to identify themselves as women at a certain point in their lives? To answer this, the Jewish community developed the feminine counterpart to Bar Mitzvah known as Bat Mitzvah, in the early 20th century. So what do the rest of us have? What are the current markers for a girl's transition into adulthood?

Well, there is the "Sweet 16" celebration many people practice. There is also the Latina "Quinceanera" celebration, as well as the "Cotillion," which is popular in the south. All of these ceremonies are ways people have adopted to mark the coming of age of a young lady. Apparently, as a society we seem to know the importance of transitioning into adulthood. However, do these celebrations genuinely mean that the threshold leading to adult ways of *being* has definitively been crossed? What are "adult ways of being" anyway? And what does a ceremonial rite of passage into adulthood have to do with MY PANTIES? Hang on girl—we're going somewhere with this.

What Paul has identified in 1st Corinthians are some key markers that I believe translate into "adult ways of being." These are: speaking, understanding and thinking. That is, an adult should be known by the way she speaks, how she understands and what she is thinking about. But why is this important? As I think about myself as an adult, and recall my childhood I can see that there have been certain ways of "being an adult" that I simply was not privy to. There were certain ways of understanding my world as a grown woman I had never encountered before. There were and are certain ways of engaging and relating to people and solving problems that I just was not aware of, nor knew how to negotiate.

I recognized that I had not progressed fully into adulthood in terms of relating to my world. When I say, "relating to my world," what I mean is: the various thought processes that encompass how I relate to people, how I understand myself, how I view and deal with challenges, among a host of other ideas that have to deal with "relating to my world."

As I continued to think about my own transition into adulthood I couldn't help thinking about the aforementioned ceremonies that have been established to mark this important passage. What bothers me is that while the ceremonies are a grand display of festivity and honor, I don't believe that they do much along the lines of informing children of what it means to be an adult.   There should be a passing-on of *useful* knowledge and *mature* character traits.

This is one main reason I chose to discuss Bar Mitzvah. You see, Bar Mitzvah simply indicates a specific point in time whereby all things *childish* (unuseful, immature) must cease in the life of a young person.   There are specific things that young Jewish men HAD to know: certain verses of scripture, certain historical knowledge, and certain ways of carrying oneself.   All of these aspects combined marked the difference between a boy and a man.   The most important ingredient was KNOWLEDGE along with the understanding and application of it.   I don't see this transfer of knowledge, understanding and character traits taking place in our society today.   I see grown women relating to their world as children, not adults.   There are women still wearing their little girl panties.

When I was a little girl I had panties that displayed my favorite cartoon characters, the days of the week, and even the alphabet.   However, when I became a teenager, not only did those panties not fit me anymore, but they no longer appealed to me either.   My preferences had changed.   I had outgrown my former stage of life.   I came to an age where I had to destroy those unuseful panties; or at least put them away never to be touched again.

In terms of me as an adult, my preferences have changed even more.   First of all, I certainly cannot fit any panties that I wore as an adolescent.   In addition, I have also learned that panties really do serve a healthful purpose, especially for women. I cannot wear thongs all week long.   I cannot wear lace panties over and over.   NO—my feminine genitalia, as does yours, needs cotton.   Now, I certainly am not saying that thongs or lacy womanly panties are somehow inappropriate, but they cannot be worn for all occasions.   Our feminine bodies are constantly draining fluids. For me to go day after day wearing thongs because "I don't want any panty lines to show," would be an invitation for infection of some extreme uncomfortable sort. I had to learn which panties were useful to me and why as well as *when*. I had to learn that cute and sexy is not always sanitary. I had to allow my knowledge as an adult woman to change my practices from childish and unlearned to mature and well informed.

In most cases this "knowledge" came by way of trial and error, not by way of parental transfer. Unlike young Jewish men or women, I had no such celebration, cultural awareness or transition period. Many ways of speaking as an adult, or thinking as an adult, and certainly understanding as an adult were completely alien to me. And I don't think I'm the only woman to admit this. I don't think that we seriously discuss maturity and what it really entails for the lives of young women. How is maturity gauged? When do we know for sure that we are operating in adulthood? And when do we know that we are doing that effectively?

This notion of entering into adulthood presents yet another area of lack that exists among many women. Having already discussed my problem of not having any sound feminine role models, it's fairly easy to see that certain "adult ways of being" could also be absent in the lives of many women. So what's the answer for this? The bible says, *"Older women likewise are to be reverent in behavior . . . they are to teach what is good"* (Titus 2:3 ESV). The next verse says, *"That they (older women) must [teach] younger women to be sober-minded"* (Titus 2:4 YLT). These verses are basically saying that there should be identifying markers in the lives of "older women," such as reverent or respectable behavior. Also, they should have some store of knowledge that they are "teaching" and passing on to the next generation of women. But where are these "older women?" And who is teaching the younger women?

We have generations of women who not only have to learn how to be feminine, but they also need to learn how to be *grown* women who are mature and operate in wisdom. When women in their 50s are dating men in their 20s, and this activity is endorsed by the society in which we live, "Houston we have a problem." When women are scantily dressed in church pews, leading worship & praise, or even preaching the gospel, we are telling our girls that their bodies are for show-and-tell. We are creating a misinformed generation of "Girls Gone Wild."

The real issue is the THINKING, or lack thereof, behind the behavior, the KNOWLEDGE that drives the actions. When I consider this idea of maturation I can't help but think of King Solomon. He is still considered the world's wealthiest and wisest king that ever lived. He is often noted for the famous request that He made of God. Solomon says, *"Give me wisdom and knowledge, that I may lead this people, for who is able to govern this great people of Yours?"* (2 Chronicles 1:10 NIV). Solomon didn't just ask God for *wisdom*. He asked God for wisdom AND knowledge *to lead His people*. He asked God to instill within him the tools he needed to properly relate to those under his care. King Solomon, essentially, asked God to grow him up in his thinking and in the ways he related to his world.

If we look at the life of Solomon we can certainly conclude that his request was not an unreasonable one. He watched his father, King David, relate to his family and his kingdom in different ways. Under the rule of his father, Solomon witnessed the rape and humiliation of his sister Tamar. He witnessed his brother chasing his father out of the kingdom. He witnessed one brother murder another.

He witnessed a household full of dysfunction. Yeah—I think asking God for wisdom and knowledge was definitely in order for King Solomon. But that's not all. In the above verse the original language speaks of "going out and coming in before the people." This denotes a person's conduct and behavior in front of others. That is, Solomon was concerned about his actions. He was asking God to give him *wisdom* and *knowledge* in order that his *behavior* would be appropriate to lead the people.

Apparently, the wisdom and knowledge that we have determines our behavior. If we are going to behave as adults we must have adult knowledge and understanding. If we don't have useful knowledge that can serve us in adulthood we are operating in childish knowledge that is un-useful to us and to those who are watching our lives to determine how to live theirs. All of this goes back to the idea of childish ways of knowing and understanding versus adult ways of knowing and understanding.

In order to move fully into adulthood we have to do as Paul has said and DESTROY, or "put away," the childish ways of knowing and understanding. However, we must first be able to identify what constitutes childish ways of knowing and understanding.

Children expect someone else to cater to their needs. They see things they want and reach for them without asking. Children don't understand the concept of time. They have to learn how to wait before something is given to them. They have to learn self-control. Children want to always be given and are seldom willing to give. Children get their feelings hurt and no longer want to be friends. Children only care about their own points of view.

One major identifying marker of childishness is selfishness. As a parent, one thing I can certainly attest to is the innate selfishness of children. They are literally born knowing how to be selfish—and in truth, they cannot help it. A crying baby is thinking about himself needing comfort or food, and by all reasonable rights he should be. A mother's main role is to absolutely meet those natural "selfish" needs of her child. But at a certain age, the mother must help that child transition into self-sufficiency. Where a mother once held the baby's bottle for him, his little limbs have developed enough to be able to hold his own bottle. The mother's role is being constantly curtailed, as it should be. That is, certain childish ways of being are constantly being "put away" as children grow up. Or at least, they should be.

All of these childish markers have a tendency to follow

WHERE I LEFT MY PANTIES

us into adulthood when they have not been put away and exchanged for adult ways of being.   This is where we need to do as King Solomon did and ask God for wisdom and knowledge.   We need to first ask God to reveal in us anything that has not fully matured in our lives.   We need to ask God what an adult woman is supposed to sound like, think like, understand like, and look like.   When Solomon asked God for the wisdom and knowledge to lead, he was making the declaration that he did not know what he was doing.   He recognized that he needed help.

This is probably the main mark of maturation.   The bible says in James 1:5, *"If you need wisdom, ask our generous God, who gives to all liberally, and He will give it to you.   He will not rebuke you for asking"* (NKJV NLT).   God is well aware that there are things we simply do not know nor know how to do. But there must come a point in our lives where we are willing to seek this information out and learn what we don't know.

I believe that God has a designated time period for each of us that pushes us into adulthood.   Or rather, things take place in our lives that force us to *speak* differently, *understand* differently, *dress* differently and *think* differently.   For many of us catastrophe is what pushes into adulthood; it's metamorphic. We go through a traumatic experience and come out on the other side forever changed—either for good or bad.   That's what happened to me with "old friend."

The devastation that I endured changed me forever, and

had the potential to stunt my growth.   I could have stayed right where that man had left me—in a ditch filled with darkness unwilling to climb out, trapped in a childish pattern of relating to my world and to men.   Thankfully, I am constantly learning new knowledge and wisdom about who I am, but this is not always the case.   Many of us go through trauma and are stunted by it.   Pain can shut down all of our faculties, leave us in unforgiveness and cause us to be unwilling to hear what we need to hear in order to grow and transform.   Simply too hurt to move toward maturing in our emotions and the way we relate to our world.

In my youth I met a boy who represented salvation to me.   Because I was tormented by feelings of low self-esteem and needed to feel valuable to someone, this boy came along and made me feel visible, wanted, needed.   He supplied me with everything I had never known: a sense of worth, a sense of my own beauty, a sense of being affirmed.   So my heart clung to this young man.   Because I had so much lack in my life it was easy to hang on to the tidbits of value he ascribed to me.   I gladly accepted whatever made me feel good about myself.   I was a child in need.   I never felt the security of a sure identity because my identity had not been grounded on something secure, stable and solid.

That little girl never learned how to let God meet her inherent human needs.   Those being: the need to be affirmed, the need for affection, the need of attention, the need of approval and the need of acceptance.   So she grew up physically, but not emotionally or psychologically. She entered her adult years still expecting someone to come along and fulfill those needs, save her the way that young man had saved her. See her the way that young man saw her. When someone, actually that same young man, came along seemingly willing to fit the bill, again her soul latched on to a person who would eventually fail her yet again.

The truth is that we all expect someone to meet those needs; we all should have someone who does. For children it should be their parents, but when it is not a stunting of growth occurs. Children will always yearn for what they never experienced. What we lack we lust for. As we grow into adults having never had those needs met we will try to meet them ourselves. Our longing souls cry out "gimme, gimme, gimme." This is the manifestation of a childish pattern of relating that leaves us insecure about who we are. We long to be loved in ways that articulate to us that we are visible and worthy and valuable. We question whether we are any of those when our needs go unmet.

This is why we must get our needs met by Someone whose supply can't be depleted. Until our identities are established in Christ we will keep searching for someone to fill us up and tell us we are special, priceless, adored. The moment that person fails us the need within us that they filled becomes void again. We become insecure because we relied on someone else's estimation of our value. And the person we relied on was not in a position to ascribe such worth because people's opinions will often change. People are fickle that way. But there is Someone whose opinion of you will NEVER change. There is Someone whose word you can ALWAYS rely on. Only Jesus can ascribe you value and worth that is unchangeable *no matter what you do* because HE is unchangeable. *He changes not* (Malachi 3:6). *He never changes His mind* (Romans 11:29). *And when He is for you He is ALL IN* (James 1:17).

In order to enter maturity we must first recognize that Jesus has everything we need. We have to come to Him with what we have and exchange it for what He has. The process of entering maturity is an exchange of all our childish ways of knowing, understanding and behaving for better, adult ways of being. We must exchange our hurts for healing. We must exchange our ignorance for knowledge. We must exchange our insecurity for identity in Christ. We must exchange our selfishness for service to others. We must exchange our stubbornness for humility. We must exchange our negative perceptions for positive perspectives. We must "put away" the childish ways of being and "put on" adulthood. And yes—it's going to take time and effort on our part.

We have to recognize childish ways for what they are, and be willing to seek the knowledge that we need in order to grow and change. God is well able to give us the wisdom and knowledge we need, and He will lead us to resources that will deepen our knowledge as well. Real change happens when right knowledge and wisdom are put into practice. By practicing what is right we turn away from what is wrong. As we learn new habits and develop right behaviors, the old ones will die off on their own. The more we operate in right thinking, the less we will operate in childish thinking.

Are we going to identify ways of thinking and understanding that can't serve us as adults? Or are we going to keep trying to wear the panties that we wore as little girls? It's time to grow up. It's time to exchange the panties of immaturity for the wisdom and knowledge of God. Psalm 27:10 says, *"When my father and my mother forsake me, then The Lord will take me up."* You may not have been properly equipped to enter adulthood. You may have been stunted from growth because of pain. That's OK. Let The Lord take you up and out of the panties of your past and walk you into your future as a FULL GROWN WOMAN of God.

Chapter 8

The "Big Girl" Panties

*I*f you have made it this far through this book let me just say: THANK YOU! I'm not really sure how easy or entertaining it is to read all of this, but writing it sure has been a labor of love. I have done my best to stay true to who I really am and what I genuinely believe I have heard from God. My aim is not to paint a pretty picture for you. My aim is not to give you a five-step program on how to deal with men and hear from God or any of that jazz. My main goal was to tell my story so that someone might be helped or encouraged; and hopefully I have done that to some small degree.

When I was about half-way through this effort, God spoke to me and told me that I needed to include this last chapter as a cry for accountability. I can tell my story 'til the cows come home. You can read this book over and over ad infinitum, and in the end you will be no less free from sexual sins or soul ties or strongholds in your life than you were before. The real point is that you have to do something. Pastors can pray for you, lay hands on you, speak a word-of-wisdom over you, but unless you actually take the words of wisdom and apply them to your life, nothing is going to change. You're still going to leave your panties all over America, and your heart is still going to be broken.

So what's the good news? The only good news I have is that Jesus is alive and He loves you. When you're crying in the middle of the night because you're lonely—He loves you. When you've fallen into someone's bed and you feel like you can't get up—He loves you. When you feel like He has been withholding from you and you want to turn away from Him—Jesus still loves you. Learning how to agree with and receive His love is something else entirely. I'm not going to tell you it's easy. I'm not going to tell you any of that church cliché stuff that you've probably heard already. The absolute truth is that it's going to be HARD.

Unraveling years and years of wrong ways of thinking and BE-ing will not be overcome in a single prayer. But that sure is a great place to start.

One of the greatest things that God ever spoke to me was *"Little by Little I will drive your enemies away"* (Exodus 23:30). In the bible God says this to the children of Israel as He is explaining to them how they should conduct themselves while *in the wilderness.* At the time that God is revealing these things to Moses the Israelites are not yet in the land of Promise. They are not in their own land. They are merely sojourning through a land that would sustain them until they eventually come to the place that they will take up permanency. KEEP THAT IN MIND—you may not be at your final destination, but in THIS PLACE God has a plan of providence for you.

God was essentially establishing their borders and explaining some mandates to them while they were on their way. Because they had recently been delivered from extreme bondage, it was important to God that they have a season of reestablishing their sense of humanity. That is not to say that the Israelites were uncivilized or anything like that. But having been under so much oppression, I believe God wanted to reteach them how to live under HIS authority versus the oppression of a slavemaster.

In this crucial time period and in this land of visitation God was not silent on the fact that they would encounter enemies. He makes it very clear to the Israelites that enemies are going to come from the north, the south, the east and the west. The good news for them was that GOD WAS WITH THEM, and He was at this critical time promising never to leave them alone or defenseless. So as a means of reassurance, God says to the Israelites of their enemies, *"Little by little I will drive them (enemies) out from before you until you have increased and you inherit the land"* (Exodus 23:30 NKJV emphasis mine).

What in the world does that mean? To understand this verse we have to go to the one right before it which says, *"I will not drive them (enemies) out from before you in one year, lest the land become desolate and the beasts of the field become too numerous for you"* (Exodus 23:29). God is saying that if He were to destroy every enemy of Israel all at once a famine would soon follow and LIFE would overtake them. You see, the translation for the word "beast" in this verse is actually "life," meaning: anything living—plant life, animal life or even LIFE ITSELF. God knows and understands that we can be overwhelmed with life.

Not only that, but when nothing is opposing us idleness can set in and cause us to get a little too comfortable. And when we are comfortable and idle what do you think is going to happen once we are confronted with real danger? As weird as this is going to sound, God happens to know that enemies are necessary. The Israelites needed an opposing force to strengthen them for encountering a real battle. In addition, their enemies were essential in subduing the land as well. Their enemies were needed in order to maintain the balance of life. The enemies of Israel also had a share to partake in with the maintenance of the land that they were all living in. I'm sure this doesn't sound encouraging, but you need enemies. Enemies will show you your strengths and your weaknesses. God is wise enough to know how to utilize our enemies to our greatest advantage.

You need to know that broken heartedness is an enemy. Loneliness is an enemy. Bondage is an enemy. Wrongful soul-ties are enemies. All of these unhealthy states-of-being mean you nothing but harm all the days of your life and they absolutely mean to destroy you. But trust me—they are all necessary for your strength and growth. The unfortunate truth is that all of these enemies aren't just going to leave because you don't want them around or because you ignore them. On the contrary, they must be acknowledged and they must be driven away, and that is God's job with your cooperation. But He does this little by little—not all at once—because your enemies are meant to grow you.

Understanding the reason why "all at once" is not beneficial to us is paramount. Careful study of Exodus 23:30 reveal that God's intention was to slowly allow the Israelites to become strong enough to possess their own land. God's job was to fend off the enemies that they were not yet prepared to fight against. His job was to allow them to reproduce or bear fruit ("increase") until they were ready to possess ("inherit") their own land. Their job was to learn how to take possession of the land.

Taking possession is not about simply occupying space. It's about knowing: how to work the land, how to defend the land, how to care for the land, how to maintain the land. It was their job to learn how to take possession of the land so that when God was ready to give them their full inheritance they were equipped to handle it both physically and mentally.

God had a part to play and the Israelites had a part to play as well. They had to cooperate with God. In like manner, we have to give Him the permission and opportunity to do His part in our lives. We must cooperate with God, but we must also be willing to learn and do our part.

What does that look like? It looks like allowing God a space in our lives—acknowledging that we do not know everything and we need help. It looks like being honest with who we really are and where we really are—recognizing our weaknesses and being willing to learn from them. It looks like fighting through the pain of our past and present while seeking to understand the why about it all.

Giving God permission to invade our lives looks like taking a small step toward Him. It looks like agreeing with Him that sinful patterns are not His best for us. It looks like faith—believing in Who God really is and Who He wants to be to us. It looks like hope—agreeing that we really can be who God says that we are. And it looks like love—understanding that God's love for us is not based on anything that we do or don't do. Faith, Hope and Love are the necessary ingredients to cooperate with God and wage a successful war against our adversaries.

And here's a fact: you can't wage war on an enemy that you don't know exists. God can't drive away something that you are unwilling to admit is there. This is where accountability comes in. Accountability is about acknowledgement and taking responsibility. It's about the "what" that has happened; not necessarily the "why." Merriam-Webster defines accountability as: "the quality or state of being accountable, *especially*: an obligation or willingness to accept responsibility or to account for one's actions" (emphasis NOT mine in this case but Merriam Webster's). To further understand this definition, you should also understand that "accountable" means "answerable."

In other words, to be accountable is to give an answer for your actions. I would say that to be accountable is to own your actions—whether good or bad. Accountable, to me, and in the context of this book, means to at least be willing to take responsibility for whatever actions you take or have taken.

When I was studying for this section, I hit a wall in regard to accountability. Mainly because I know some people confuse accountable with guilt. I have three children: two teenage daughters and a kindergartener. When I have to leave them alone my oldest teenager is in charge. She is responsible for her younger siblings. If something funky happens while I'm out, say, Alonzo breaks into the freezer and eats a tub-load of ice cream, I am going to hold my oldest daughter *responsible* for what has happened even though she is not guilty.

Just listen to me for a moment. Her brother would be punished, but she would have to give an *answer* as to why she allowed him to behave in such a way. And "I don't know" is never a suitable answer in my home. As the person in charge, my oldest daughter would have to give an account of her position as leader and how she didn't manage it well. She may or may not be punished for her lack of positive control of her brother while I was away. She is responsible but not guilty of the offense. She must give an account or record of the details involved with the offense but she is only taking responsibility for her actions or non-actions in this case.

This is what I believe God wants us to know about accountability: while we may not be the perpetrators of the wrongs we have experienced we are still accountable to God for who we are because of them. We can still give an account for the details of our lives with the understanding that we are not necessarily guilty. And then of course there may be some things that we absolutely are guilty of. We take responsibility for ALL of those things by acknowledging them to God and being willing to give an answer for them. It is only when we can acknowledge our own areas of responsibility that God can move in to fight on our behalf.

In the example that I just gave, had my daughter said, "I don't know" when asked "What happened here?" I would not have been able to fight on her behalf. She was in charge and she has no answer to give me about the ones she was in charge of? That is not a good look.   Now on the other hand, if she comes to me and gives me the details of the situation, say, something along the lines of, "Mom I was in the bathroom and I told Alonzo to sit and watch TV.   When I came out I found him sticky-handed."   This gives me something to work with.   I can now move in and fight on her behalf.   I can issue the correct punishment to her brother who represents an enemy to her status as leader right now.   I can admonish him that "when I am away big sis is in charge" and so forth.   Without the step of responsibility on my daughter's part she would likewise be numbered with her brother who is going to feel the wrath of the returning Queen of the castle.

This is how God needs to be able to fight for us.   But He is rendered incapable when we won't acknowledge the details. And those details may be just as sticky as a five-year-old who ransacked the freezer for some ice cream.   Those details may be full of things you absolutely could not prevent from happening. Those details of your lives may be hurtful to recall but they must be accounted for.   They need to be answered.   And "I don't know what happened," will not suffice because you do know. You know that Mr. Wrong broke your heart.   You know that you gave that man your panties.   You know that your mother made you feel unloved.   You know that your father was not visible.   You know that when you're lonely you just want to be held and caressed.   You know the details.   But if you want to fight against the enemies that threaten your security you need to account for them.

195

Alone, we are powerless to fight our enemies—that is, if we really believe that we are alone. I know how it feels to be lonely. Loneliness is a fact and a horrible feeling that drives you into behaviors and thought patterns that contradict who you really are. Loneliness is a driver—a slavemaster. It is loneliness that causes a woman to give her panties to man after man after man KNOWING that she is so much better than that. But being alone is not a truth. Hear me—I am in no way minimizing what you genuinely feel. Your feelings are important to God. You being alone and feeling alone is important to God. In fact, you being alone is the FIRST thing that God ever said was NOT good (Genesis 2:18). The truth, however, is that we are not alone even when we feel like we are. Even when it looks like we are. And trust me, if you're single and have been for many years, you're going to feel alone.

The difficulty for us is to believe what God has said versus what we see and feel. It is difficult to believe that God is for us when everything seems to be coming against us. It is difficult to believe that we are precious and special to God when everyone we have ever known has made us feel like crap. It is difficult to believe that God is with us when we are surrounded by foes. It is difficult to believe that we are lovable when we have been rejected to no end. I know it's difficult to believe. I have struggled with it many times in my life—and not too long ago either. Even after God has shown up in major ways for me I still sometimes struggle to believe that He is with me.

This is the tough part.   You and I have a choice to make in the midst of what is visible and what is invisible.   Will we only believe everything that we can see?   Or will we rise to the point of genuine authentic trust and believe what we cannot see? Our basic profession of faith in God is an admission of belief in Someone unseen.   If you have taken that step, certainly, you can take another just like it.   We have to knuckle-up and CHOOSE to believe despite what we see or how we feel.

Faith isn't based on what things look like.   By its very description, faith has to be based on something unseen.   *"Now faith is the substance of things HOPED for, the evidence of things NOT seen"* (Hebrews 11:1, emphasis mine).   If something is unseen it is also unfelt.   We have to do the work of believing in order to see and experience real change.   Trust me; we are going to be fought at every turn.   We are going to be attacked by a host of enemies.   Even in that, we must still choose to partner with God and allow Him to drive our enemies away. . . . . little by little.

We partner with Him when we believe Him, and we show that we believe Him by trusting Him when we can't see or feel Him.   I am sure that all of this believing and trusting sounds simple, but when you have had your heart broken time and time again by Mr. Wrong, and have had life kick you while you're down, believing and trusting God is the last thing on your mind—I know that place all too well.

If you take a good long gander at the book of Psalms you will see what I mean. David struggled with doubting God. Oh yes he did too!! That's right—the "man after God's own heart" struggled to believe the things God had told him about his future, about his identity and about his struggles in life. David had to talk himself into believing God. Here is David's reality: a son who tried to kill him, a daughter raped by her brother, a friend who killed his son (David's son), guilty of adultery and murder, and a nation that had turned its back on him. You don't think the question, "am I really cut out for this?" ever crossed King David's mind? You don't think the question, "God are you still on my side?" ever presented itself to David? You don't think the question "Lord, am I still worthy?" was ever at the forefront of his mind? You better believe it did! Many of the Psalms of David are confessions or attempts to encourage himself in the midst of a divided confidence in God.

If it happened to King David, why wouldn't it happen to us?

Your real enemy, the devil, is the master of the principle "divide and conquer." If he can get you feeling and believing that you are alone, you won't take action. You will sit around and stew on the FACT that you are alone and never operate in the TRUTH that you are not. The devil will even create a division within yourself. If your *mind* is unwilling to recognize the truth of God, your *mouth* will do the same, resulting in your body and soul (the part of you that houses your mind) making a majority ruling against your spirit, which is the only part of you that is like God. In the end, you will find yourself unable to fully trust God, and in that place of distrust you will not access genuine confidence in God that generates faith.

The devil knows all of this and has spent countless generations perfecting his craft. He knows all too well how to get BELIEVERS to stop doing what they were created to do—believe. He does this by ensuring that you feel alone and isolated. And you feel the most alone when you have been disappointed—by the people that you expected to love you, by the people that you have poured your own love out for, even by God Himself. Oh yes—you can certainly feel like God has let you down. If you are one of the "terminally single," as I like to call us, I know you feel let down by God—I sure did, and being very honest, sometimes I still do. When you feel let-down you are not in a place of action. You are in a place of sorrow. In that sorrow there is no movement, only the stillness of a wounded heart trying desperately to mend itself and comprehend all the hurt.

The sad truth is that we may never fully understand all the hurts that we have suffered. We may never get the answers to the whys of our lives. God never promised us answers to everything that happens to us. That sucks! I know it does because I agree. But this is where we move from being people who feel like God has mistreated us to being people who can readily accept that God is greater than we; and this is a matter of CHOICE. It is a matter of our thinking.

When Job had lost literally everything except his life his wife told him to curse God and die. *Job replied, "shall we indeed (only) accept good from God and not accept adversity?"* (Job 2:10 NASB) We need to interrogate ourselves in the same manner. What do we believe about God? Do we believe that He is good? Do we believe that He is worthy to be trusted when we don't understand? Or do we believe that the moment He disappoints us—does not live up to OUR expectations and time frames—He is no longer deserving of our trust? These are questions we must be willing to engage ourselves in. We must be willing to challenge our thinking, and not simply challenge it but also CHANGE it.

You know, Job gets a pretty bad rep. Many a Christian is convinced of Job's unbelief and fear being the culprit behind his suffering. I just cannot accept that as true. We can certainly INFER that those are the reasons for his being tested, but that isn't what the bible says expressly. God is up in heaven bragging about how great of a guy Job is. God is genuinely impressed with him. Nowhere in the conversation with the devil does God have an aside and question Job's faith; the fact that the church does is beyond me. It's akin to saying that Job does not have a right to feel bad about the extreme loss he has undergone.

The guy lost ALL of his children, ALL of his livestock and ALL of his money—get this: ALL IN ONE DAY! And you want to tell me that he doesn't have a right to mourn?! You really expect me to believe that his statement in verse 25 of

200

chapter 3: *"The thing that I feared the most has come upon me" is somehow a revelation that Job was overly fearful?"* So if all of your children die in a horrible car accident RIGHT NOW and as you're trying to synthesize that news your car gets stolen, your home burns to the ground, the bank holding all of your money crashes, and the people who have known you for years having only witnessed GOOD from you accuse you of EVIL, you mean to tell me that these events are going to lead you into counting it all joy??? I seriously doubt that. You are going to be stunned to your core. Even if you are super saint baptized in The Holy Ghost with the evidence of speaking in tongues you are going to have a moment or two of some real grief. AND THAT'S OK. It's OK with God. So why isn't it Ok with us?

I think the real beauty of the story about Job is not that he suffered so much and in the end "got double for his trouble." Don't get me wrong, that's certainly absolutely God's intention for any of us who have suffered. However, we have been conditioned to pay so much attention to the restoration of his STUFF, that we miss the restoration of his SIGHT. Beyond the return of his things, Job has a gynormous revelation at the close of his story.

The real beauty for me was the authentic transformation of his mind and his heart in the process. After God has interrogated him about the beginning of time and all of creation, Job makes one final statement that impresses me to literal dumbfoundedness. He says, *"I had only heard of you by hearing of the ear, but now my eyes SEE YOU"* (Job 42:5 emphasis

201

mine). WHOA!! That's so deep you can't even measure it. This was the real victory; but the very next verse is also of keen importance. Job goes on to say: *"Therefore I retract, and I REPENT in dust and ashes"* (Job 42:6 NASB). Now, I could go on and break down this verse to its literal meaning, but the most important word here is REPENT. It was only when Job saw God for Who He authentically is that Job's heart and mind and VISION were changed forever.

The word REPENTENCE gets muddied, misinterpreted and mishandled by the church world. The absolute definition of REPENT is TO CHANGE ONE'S MIND. We have heard many, many Christian leaders say of "repent" something like: "a full one hundred and eighty degree turn in the other direction." That sounds real good, and certainly changing one's direction is advantageous and will take place eventually. But that is NOT what that word means.

Truly, once a person can recognize the truth about something, then she may be able to turn from her ways because now she understands that her ways of doing and being and thinking are not consistent with living a life that pleases God. But all of that changing of behavior will not take place until an authentic and genuine change of thinking and SEEING takes place FIRST.

Suppose I had grown up in a society that told me I need to have sex with every man that I date because that is how I will know if he is the man I want to spend the rest of my life with.

Then that is what would be true for me. My thinking would be shaped by this principle. My actions would be directed by this principle. Consequently, when I come into the knowledge of a genuine truth that challenges and conflicts with what I have been shaped to believe and live by, I would then be at a point of decision. I would have to decide which of the ways of thinking the genuine truth is, and which the erroneous truth is. I would have to SEE the value of the authentic truth. I would have to completely regard as false all that I had been taught, and recognize the detriment of the error that conflicts with the genuine truth.

My entire way of *thinking* would have to CHANGE. And by necessity, my entire way of BELIEVING would likewise have to change. And by consequence, the way I SEE my world would be forever changed. In order for me to accept as truth that engaging in sexual activity outside of marriage is an unacceptable way to live, I would have to really genuinely believe that God's way of living is better, or at least *agree* that it is. And the act of believing is an act of the mind in concert with the heart.

My mind is responsible for agreeing with truth and disregarding error; but my heart is responsible for taking what I agree with and making it real to me, making me believe it passionately. This is the genuine process of repentance. But believe me when I say this: it doesn't happen in one prayer. It doesn't happen in one instant. It certainly doesn't happen overnight. True repentance—a changing of the mind—could take years.

Understanding the true nature and essence of genuine repentance is so paramount. It is of extreme importance to recognize that authentic repentance takes place in the mind FIRST. Only when one changes her mind can one change her actions.

What does any of this have to do with my panties, or man issues or "self" issues? EVERYTHING—because none of the former will change unless your mind changes first. And our minds won't change unless our words change. It is our words that lead our thinking. Just like you can talk yourself out of doing something, you can also talk yourself IN to doing something—even thinking the right way. The bible says, *"Let the weak SAY I am strong," "I will SAY of The Lord he is my refuge," "Let the redeemed of The Lord SAY so"* (Joel 3:10, Ps 91:2, Ps 107:2 respectively). All of these acknowledgements point to the power of our words to shape our thinking. What was it that David was doing throughout most of the Psalms? Speaking to himself in order to fully convince himself of whatever he was saying.

I fully believe that in times of extreme bondage and brokenness, the only ACT of faith required is the mere exertion of your vocal chords by SAYing something. Here's some more truth: sometimes that's all you CAN do is SAY something. Even when it is half-hearted and seemingly ingenuine, I think God honors the small step toward Him. I can personally attest to some half-hearted confessions of faith that resulted in God's power still showing up for me.

After all, we're talking about the same God who says that the only amount of faith necessary to move a mountain is as small as a seed that can be held in your hand (Matt 17:20). If this is true (and it is), then genuine faith must not be wrapped up in complete trust. If faith is nearly invisible to the human eye, it must have a little bit of doubt along with it too. And I cringe to say that. I am certainly not saying that doubting God is something you want to practice; that's not at all what I am implying here. I am simply saying that I believe God is well aware that our faith in Him can be mixed with some doubt on our part.

And truthfully, I don't think that "doubt" is the proper word; I believe the proper term is "wonder." We *wonder* if what we believe will really manifest. We *wonder* if God is really going to answer us. And if He answers, we *wonder* if it's going to be what we hoped it would. I don't think God is put off by our small measure of faith tinged with sincere wonder that could be misconstrued as doubt or unbelief to others. God is able to take that tiny seed of faith and grow it into a full-grown tree by responding to our small acts of faith.

Seeing and experiencing God when He responds to our small faith is what causes are faith to move from the seed to the tree.

We have to start somewhere. We have to begin with the small things that we are capable of doing; and the one small thing that we can absolutely do is SPEAK. When we don't feel like it's making a difference. When we can't see the effects of it, we can take the small step of faith and talk ourselves into thinking differently. The importance of doing this lies in the truth about how God responds to us. God says in Matthew 18:19, *"if any two of you shall agree on earth as touching (concerning) anything that they shall ask, it shall be done for them of my Father which is in heaven."* To understand this principle as it relates to us personally we need to keep in mind that we are three-part beings, as I discussed earlier. We are spirits that have souls and we live in bodies. The aim is to get all of these parts of who we are to be aligned—in agreement—so that God can manifest what we agree to.

Our spirit wants and desires to remain connected to God. When we ignore our spirit's cravings, we ignore the part of us that is like God, and in a small way we ignore God too. The parts of us that are responsible for everything we do in life are our souls and bodies; we function in life by way of these. If we take our bodies and align them with our spirit we will create an "agreement" within ourselves. How do we do this? We use the one part of our body that we can consciously control—our mouths. When our mouths in agreement with our spirits we successfully create a majority that can override even our minds or our thinking.

In fact, this is the only way to override our thinking. And here is the amazing part: we don't have to start off with full-fledged belief of the things that we speak. We simply *agree* that what we are speaking is TRUE, and we speak them and speak them UNTIL we are convinced of their truth because that is the principle of agreement at work also. Our mouth is agreeing with our spirit and God's word and those TWO OR THREE coming together results in God doing whatever they are agreeing to.

Our constant speaking and speaking is not a vain exercise. It seems rote and fruitless because we can't see what our words are actually doing—just like we can't see God with our human eyes (although I do believe there are exceptions to even this). Our words, especially when we are speaking The Word of God, are being agreed to by The Holy Spirit. He lives on the inside of you if you are saved. He is always there, present with you, so you are not just speaking empty senseless words into a vacuum.

You are speaking words of life that are being energized and activated by The Holy Spirit. You might not feel a thing. You might see a thing. But that in no way means that it is not working. Your words, spoken out of your mouth that are from God's own Word inevitably agreed to by The Holy Spirit, because God cannot disagree with Himself, creates the majority ruling. So what's the end result? MANIFESTATION of whatever you are speaking. That is, God's power changes your mind.

207

And let me insert this one thing for good measure: I HAVE NOT ARRIVED! I have not mastered this concept completely myself. I am just like you. Many times I wonder myself if God is going to answer and how. I feel like my words aren't accomplishing anything at times. But I have something to hold on to; I have a record of God's faithfulness to me in times of complete distress. I remind myself of how God came through for me when no one was there to help me. I remind myself of times when I was speaking and declaring something and at the same time still wondering if it was going to work—IT DID. That is how I draw hope—by reminding myself of what God has already done in my life. I remind myself of God's word when it uniquely meets me at the particular crossroad that I may be at. *God said that my HOPE cannot leave me disappointed* (Romans 5:5). So I take my HOPE and mix it with my mustard seed of faith and wait it out. That's all I can do. That's all WE can do.

And many times you're gonna feel like a dang fool too. You are going to look around at every one else receiving their promises and wonder "WHAT ABOUT ME???" You see, while God has shown up and showed out countless times on my behalf there are times when all of my proclaiming and declaring and decreeing affected NOTHING on my behalf. Go ahead and get that indifferent puzzled look off of your face. YES—God's answer really can be NO. Let me go ahead and make it all the way real—I am a single woman in her thirties still waiting to be found by some man who will love and honor me as his wife. And I don't even have any good possibles. Sometimes—MANY times what I was declaring did not manifest as I thought it should have. We're at the end now so you may as well know the complete unadulterated NAKED TRUTH.

So what did I do with that? Well, I was mad. Mmm hmm—at GOD. I have had many times where I found myself at ought with God. Times where I was offended with Him. I felt so betrayed by Him. I grew a little callous toward God and a little distrustful of Him because of it. I felt like He was no longer on my side.

How did I get over that? It was difficult to be quite honest. I had to realize that God, first and foremost, is not like me. His ways of doing and thinking really are unfathomably higher than mine as He Himself explains in the bible (Isaiah 55:9). I had to also understand that God may have simply wanted me to learn more about myself in the process, say, for instance, my inclination to judge Him as unfaithful the moment I don't get my way.

I had to learn that there are things about God I will *always* NEVER know (yeah, I meant to say it exactly the way you read it). There will be things in life I will not have an answer to. But in the bigger broader beautiful picture of my life I have got to see God as good. I must determine within myself to view God as good no matter the outcome in my life. I have to be willing to recount all the good that God has ever shown me and count it enough simply because He is not bound by my estimation of good. God's goodness cannot be measured by my finite mind.

We're talking about God who spared the lives of the very first sinners simply because He could. And I want to ascribe Him as less than good because He didn't do what I thought He *should* have done for ME? Shame on me.

When I think about Job and the extreme gravity of all that he had endured and never once accused God of doing him wrong, who am I? Job's story is intensely more profound than we have really understood it to be. He didn't simply repent to God and chock it all up to a misunderstanding on his part. Job was completely utterly esoterically transformed. He suffered tremendously—God actually chose him to suffer. And right before he repents, the change in him is clearly evident. Job is keenly aware of Who God REALLY is.

I have studied and studied the first four verses of Job 42, and what God has revealed to me about their true meaning, based on the original language, is truly breathtaking. It is these first verses of the chapter that set up the restoration of Job's whole life. In verse 2 Job recalls that God really can do anything. But Job goes on to say that not even "thoughts" can be hidden from God. The importance of this lies in the next verse. Job says in verse 3, *"Who is he that hides counsel without knowledge? I HAVE UTTERED."* You see, when God firsts responds to Job's condition, He poses this question to Job. The indication here is that Job must have been THINKING this, but had not spoken it. In a way, Job was expressing some offense toward God. But he never verbalized it. So when God exposes to Job the hidden intents of his heart, he is undone by

210

the fact that God even knows *that* and yet spares his life.

This one particular verse, Job 42:4, is the fulcrum of the story for me. It reads, *"Hear, I beseech thee. I will speak. I will demand of thee and declare thou unto me."* This verse is not saying "now I'm going to demand of YOU God since you have been demanding me to answer you." It could be misinterpreted that way when you don't know the original language and you fail to realize the weight of the situation as it is between God and Job at this point. In this verse the actual literal translation is "Hear me, I beg you. I PROMISE I will ask You and You CAUSE ME TO KNOW." God allowed so much torment, so much pain, so much loss, so much heartache, so much hell in Job's life for the express purpose of getting Job TO ASK HIM. And not just ask but to also be in a place where God could MAKE KNOWN to him.

Ask what? Whatever you do not know. Make what known? HIMSELF. God makes Himself known to us when we ask. And sometimes when we don't ask He causes us to know Him through our suffering. That's where I found out Who God really is. When I suffered like I hadn't suffered in all of my life—God caused me to KNOW Him.

Job had to lose absolutely everything in his life in order to see God. Upon seeing Him he realized that he really didn't have anything to begin with that was worth keeping in comparison to Who God is. I lost a lot. I gave my panties to the wrong men on various occasions. And when I lost what I thought meant the world to me I realized my world was in the wrong place. I am learning to live with an ever ready consciousness that Jesus really is the only Man I need in my life. That doesn't mean that I don't want another man in my life—of course I do. But it does mean that I have to look to Jesus, who will never fail me, to get my needs met. It took some left turns to get here. It took some side trips, some scenic routes, even some complete stops. But on this journey I am confident that God is with me. When I can't distinguish his presence I ask Him to "cause me to know" that He is there.

So what is the absolute bottom line right now? I am not the same person I used to be. I have been wounded in battle. Left for dead. Encompassed by enemies that meant to destroy me. Some of these enemies I welcomed into my life because they appeared to be friends. Others of these enemies just kind of showed up at an inopportune time in my life. And even still other enemies were waiting until the perfect time to catch me when I was down; those were the ones who were there all the time—watching from afar waiting for me to crack.

And when I did, it seemed like even God had left me. In that place is where God had to "cause me to know" Him for real. In that place of broken dreams, deferred hopes and dwindling faith God showed me His authentic character. And by consequence He showed me who I really am. He is still showing me who I am destined to be.

Little by little God is restoring me back to life, just like

Job. You see, the end of Job's story was actually another beginning. Though he got back more than what he started off with, it didn't happen overnight. His crops didn't spring forth over night. His children weren't born one day and flourishing in the land overnight. His spouse was not found for him overnight. NO. Job had to wait the seasons out. Little by little he began to see the restoration coming back to his life. Little by little he watched his children grow and become strong in the land again. Little by little Job had to take possession of his land again. And Little by little God was able to distribute to Job his full inheritance.

In my Little-by-Little, I had to learn how to love God again. I had to learn how to love me again. I am still learning. What will you do in your season of Little-by-Little?

I may have left my panties in Florida,

my wallet in El Segundo, and my heart buried at

Wounded Knee

but what I found was myself in the genuine embrace of

God's sincere love for me.

I don't know where you left your panties, you yourself

may not be privy

but leave them right where they are and let God show

you Who He is

and by necessity who you were meant to be.

"Fear not; you will no longer live in shame.

You will not be humiliated or disgraced.

There is no more dishonor for you.

You shall forget the shame of your youth.

And no longer will you remember the scorn

and contempt of your widowhood."

Love
ALWAYS,
your Father.

An inspired interpretation of Isaiah 54:4
Based on the New Living Translation
and the New International Version of the bible.

www.ingramcontent.com/pod-product-compliance
Lightning Source LLC
Chambersburg PA
CBHW030922090426
42737CB00007B/281